he put my bddha in the freezer

The Hopes, Letdowns & Disastrous Almost-Love Stories
Of One Woman's Hollywood Decade

AMY KARL

COLUMBUS, OHIO

He Put My Buddha In The Freezer: The Hopes, Letdowns & Disastrous Almost-Love Stories of One Woman's Hollywood Decade

Published by Gatekeeper Press
2167 Stringtown Rd, Suite 109
Columbus, OH 43123-2989
www.GatekeeperPress.com

ISBN (paperback): 9781642376159
eISBN: 9781642376166

DISCLAIMER

The stories in this book reflect my recollection of events. Many names have been changed and some details modified to protect the privacy of those depicted. Dialogue has been re-created from memory.

The names of the actors remain unchanged. There is no way to fictionalize the already famous and still tell my story. The scenes with them only add to their existing charm and many of the characteristics I portray are already known in the mainstream media.

For example, no one is going to be shocked that Woody Harrelson—a known rainforest activist, vegan, and hemp clothing wearer who openly advocated his use of marijuana—might actually smoke a little weed. Plus, it's (now) legal in the state of California: a member of the Union that adores and advocates free speech, especially for the underdog: me.

Hence…*He Put My Buddha In The Freezer.*

CHAKRA ONE

Richard
December 1998 - May 2001

"We engage in many defenses
against the uncomfortable feeling
of rootlessness and insecurity."
—The Aquarian Teacher

I bellied up to the bar and downed a shot of tequila. "Want to dance?" a tall, balding, Jewish man in wired-rimmed glasses asked. He looked to be in his early forties. I sucked hard on the lemon slice that came with my tequila.

"No thanks," I replied, my face probably looking as sour as the lemon.

Undeterred, he told me his name was Richard and offered to buy me another drink. Forcing a smile, I told him I was good and turned back to chat with Amanda Peet, the up-and-coming actress who'd just starred in a film where I had my first movie role. I only had a few lines, but the part was opening some doors for me.

It was 1998, and I was at New Line Cinema's Christmas party in Los Angeles with Brett, a producer I'd been dating for about eight weeks. Brett was on the verge of making a name for himself with *American Pie*. But he'd already lied to me twice, cheated on me once, and didn't have much time in his busy schedule to see me. I planned to break it off before heading back to Chicago the following day for the holidays, but he kept introducing me as his girlfriend. Like everything in L.A., this perplexed me. Hence the tequila shot. I thought back to the day, two years earlier, when the letter arrived that would change my life:

1

It was a cold, gray day in Chicago, and I was dying for another life. One that might begin within a few weeks, depending on the contents of the envelope I was holding. I looked out the bedroom window of my first-floor apartment. Thick, frosty ice covered the pane like fairy dust. Inhaling deeply, I closed my eyes and ripped open the envelope.

Congratulations! You've been accepted into the American Conservatory Theatre.

Incapable of moving, I read and reread the words. Then a tear I hadn't even realized I shed dripped onto the letter and smeared the words a little. Hopping onto my bed, I jumped up and down with reckless abandon, hollering at the top of my lungs, "I'm going to win an Academy Award! I'm going to be an actress!"

I'd spent the better part of the last four years, since graduating from college, sorting though my parents' divorce, my father's new identity—which included, or would soon include, a shiny red Corvette, a 44-foot Beneteau sailboat, and a girlfriend my age—my mom's post-divorce size two jeans, and, oh yes, what I should be doing with my life.

At least, to that last question, I now had my answer.

Several hours later, Sam, my boyfriend of the last two years, who had a key to my place, shook me awake. He looked like a J. Crew model with his gorgeous green eyes, thick, dark eyebrows, and loose curly hair. I should have wanted to get naked with him, only every time he was in bed with me, I stroked his earlobes the way a masseuse does at the end of a massage, hoping he'd fall asleep and forget about wanting other body parts stroked.

"What's this?" he asked, peeling the clutched letter off my chest. I never told him that I'd applied to acting school.

"I'm moving to California, Sam."

"Ready for that drink yet?" Richard's voice interrupted my walk down memory lane.

I saw Brett heading toward me. Sam would never have cheated on me. He may have been boring, but at least he was loyal. Looking back at Richard, I said, "I don't need a drink, but how about that dance?"

I had no idea who Richard was or what he did for a living, but when he extended his hand and led me out to the dance floor, I felt oddly protected. A few minutes into the song, Richard asked for my number.

As I was mouthing my digits to him, Brett walked up from behind and tapped me on the shoulder. I could tell by his puppy eyes that he knew I was going to dump him. I thanked Richard for the dance, and he said that he would call me, like Brett wasn't even there.

When I returned from Christmas break, ten days later, two things were outside my door: a beautiful bouquet of flowers from Richard with a note that read, "Just Because…" and a letter from Brett apologizing for all the reasons why he hadn't called me over the holiday, begging for my forgiveness, and professing his love. Richard called me first thing on New Year's Day while I was still in Chicago. He told me he hoped all my dreams would come true and asked if he could pick me up and take me to lunch that upcoming Saturday. I told him yes and gave him my address. "We're practically neighbors," he said, going on to tell me he lived less than a mile away.

I lived just below Sunset Boulevard, across from the Viper Room (the club where River Phoenix had just died), in a rundown English Tudor Style building comprised of three bungalows and a two-story building with four apartments. I rented the apartment on the second floor. The landlord told me that Marilyn Monroe had lived in the apartment across the hall from me right before being discovered. My place was only 600 square feet and in dire need of repair-- cracked tiles in the bathroom, dirty grout on the kitchen counters, and missing knobs on the vintage stove. But

I half-hoped that living in proximity to where Marilyn began her career in Hollywood foreshadowed the kind of career opportunities awaiting me.

That Saturday, Richard knocked on my door at exactly noon. I'd assumed that he'd call from the car and I'd run down. Scanning the room for any over-looked sock piles, I noticed Richard's note prominently propped up against his vase of flowers. I thought about turning it over. But then there was a second knock. Adjusting my shirt, I opened the door. Richard was wearing sleek Italian sneakers and a designer t-shirt that showcased his perfectly trim physique.

"Cute place," he said, stepping inside. "I have a tapestry from India just sitting in storage that would look great above your couch."

I told him that would be great. Other than a sofa and mission-style credenza table, I had nothing but blank walls. I grabbed my purse off the door handle to go, and Richard asked me if I'd ever been to Greystone Park. I shook my head no. He said it used to be the private residence of the Doheny Family and had been turned into a park. Not a lot of people knew about it, so he thought we could pick up some takeout from Chin Chin and have a picnic there. Apparently, it was less than a mile from my place. Doheny Street divided Beverly Hills to the imme-diate west from the beginnings of the Sunset Strip riff raff to the immediate east, where liquor stores, pizza dens, nightclubs, and billboards sprinkled every street corner. It ran perpendicular to Sunset and was just three blocks west of my apartment. Still, once you crossed Doheny, it may as well have been a different world, one that screamed "I made it."

Minutes later, Richard and I were driving down Sunset in his gold Mercedes convertible. The top was down, and the band *Air* was cranking over the stereo system. I felt like I'd arrived. Although, technically... that happened two years earlier:

> After completing the summer acting program at The American Conservatory in San Francisco, I flew back to Chicago, stuffed everything I could fit into the trunk of my Mitsubishi Gallant, and was on the road four days later. I was so excited to get to California that I didn't bother to sort out the minor details, like telling Sam I was officially breaking up with him or putting my furniture and closet full of clothes into storage. That's what moms were for. I'd make it up to her in my acceptance speech.
>
> With only two thousand dollars to my name and a few commercial credits, I thought I was in great shape. Although my mom had offered to drive with me, a big part of me felt guilty for leaving her after the divorce, and I was afraid that forcing her to endure a grueling three-day drive would only make me feel guiltier. Especially since I was

determined to do it in twelve-hour intervals. So we just hugged and cried it out in the alley next to her house. I promised to call her from the car.

Ten hours into my road trip, it occurred to me that I might be hallucinating. *Was that water ahead on the open stretch of highway?* Nope, just concrete, I realized with each passing mile. I was listening to my Counting Crows CD for the thousandth time. Fifteen empty Coke cans and a bag of Doritos littered the passenger seat. My eyelids were getting heavy. I hadn't seen an exit in miles and my gas tank was closing on empty. But my excitement to get to L.A. transcended any worry. Plus, I was in Utah. I figured if I got stuck on the side of the road, a family of eleven would eventually pass by and help me.

At sundown, as I merged onto a single-lane highway without another car in sight and a nearly empty gas tank, it occurred to me that for all the fear I'd been plagued with over the years about confronting my acting dreams, I was absolutely fearless amidst the imposing mountains that were closing in on my car. The vastness of the fire-orange sky taking its final evening bow behind the majestic curtain of Rockies in the distance reminded me of the bow I could be taking. And for the first time in as long as I could remember, I felt like anything was possible. I felt happy and inspired by what lay ahead.

I looked over at Richard—a sexy man, driving a sexy car, listening to very sexy music—and smiled.

"So, what kind of music do you listen to?" he asked.

I always felt insecure when a guy asked me this question because I'd never spent any time exploring or going deep with what kind of music I liked and didn't like. Sort of how Julia Roberts didn't know how she liked her eggs in *Runaway Bride*. I could never remember the names of musicians or bands, so I always panicked and gave generic answers. Today was no exception.

"I love what's playing," I said.

A few moments later, we approached a long drive adorned with mature trees. In the distance was a home perched on a hillside that overlooked the whole city. I'd always assumed it was a private residence. We found a parking spot below the rolling front lawn and spread out a blanket on the grass. Other picnic goers were huddled about eating, kissing, and reading. Minutes later, we were sprawled on our stomachs feeding each other Chinese noodles with chopsticks. We were such a cliché.

"So what do you do anyway?" I laughed, as Richard sucked in a noodle through rounded lips.

"I'm a literary agent at William Morris Agency."

"No kidding. WMA represents me."

"Really!" he said. I could tell he was impressed. WMA was one of the most established talent agencies in Beverly Hills. Their theatrical and literary division only represented big name actors, and it was clear nobody knew who I was. But... they also had a commercial division. I reiterated to Richard that this was the department that represented me. Although it was much less prestigious than being represented by them on the theatrical side (booking commercials often results from something as arbitrary as wearing the right color sweater or having your hair in a ponytail the day of the casting), it was a huge break for me when they had signed me several months earlier and doubled my callback ratio. "You are at WMA?" a casting agent would now ask while scouring my resume during a casting. "Be here tomorrow at noon for a callback." It was amazing what one agency's name on a resume could do.

"I didn't even know they had a commercial division," Richard said, feeding me another noodle.

Looking into Richard's eyes, I saw a different kind of man than the one I was used to. He was mature and focused and seemed really into me. Although all of this scared me, at the same time, it made me feel safe. When he leaned in and kissed me, I closed my eyes and decided to go for it.

Each gated mansion I passed was bigger than the next. I double-checked the address. *Practically neighbors, my ass.* Richard lived on the most exclusive street in the most exclusive neighborhood off Doheny in the Hollywood Hills. A lot of agents and managers in Hollywood who worked at top firms and drove nice cars lived in one-bedroom apartments. In fact, my ex, Brett, ran his successful management/production company from his tiny two-bedroom in East Hollywood.

It was the day after our picnic, and Richard invited me over to his house to play tennis. From the front, Richard's house looked like a small, single-story concrete box, no more impressive than Brett's place. Then I walked to the door and was magically buzzed into a Japanese-style courtyard that led to another door, which opened onto a 2,000-square-foot room of glass, offering stunning 360- degree views of the city and ocean. There were mahogany floors, metal light fixtures, wood sculptures, and stainless steel appliances. It looked like a museum. As I stepped inside, Richard was making his way up a winding staircase, holding a high-tech phone that I assumed had buzzed me in. "I just love technology," he said.

I felt like a Bond Girl.

I asked Richard if the house was two stories. Taking my hand, he told me it was three and led me out to a balcony that ran the entire length of the house. I approached the rail and looked out. There was a steep drop. The house was built into a hillside, but the yard below was on an acre of flat pad. To the right was an Olympic-sized pool with a Jacuzzi;

to the left, a level below the pool, there was a tennis court with basketball hoops on each side. It was like a hotel. Looking out at Catalina Island in the distance, Richard came up and wrapped his arms around me from behind. I felt his stomach press against my back as he took a satisfied breath.

"How could you think my place is cute?" I asked.

"I think everything about you is cute," he said, kissing the back of my neck.

As I lobbed my third forehand over the fence, I knew I had already broken rule number one in Hollywood: under-hype and over-deliver. I'd told Richard I was a good tennis player over our picnic, not knowing that he'd played for UCLA or had a home with a tennis court. Hitting my second backhand into the net, I knew Richard must be bored out of his mind and offered to quit. But Richard insisted we hit a few more and approached the net to offer some tips. "You just need to transfer your weight to your front foot," he said.

I was a little overwhelmed. In my world, the only sports pointer I ever got from a boyfriend while doing something athletic together came from Sam in the back bowls of Vail a few years earlier: I was terrified, in chest-deep snow, and turned to him (an expert skier) for some advice when he skied up behind me and stopped to defrost his goggles.

"I don't know how I'm going to get down this mountain." I cried.

"You just have to make it happen," he said, parallel skiing his way past me, before catching a jump and doing the splits in mid air.

Richard walked over to my side of the court and demonstrated a couple of forehand strokes. He really exaggerated putting his weight onto his front foot so I would get it. "Why don't you go back to the baseline while I feed you a few balls from the net to help you get your footwork back?" he suggested. After a few volleys, I finally hit a cross-court winner. It occurred to me that, for the first time since moving to L.A., I felt back on my game.

After tennis, Richard led me up a very steep outdoor staircase that opened to his bedroom. It had such a Zen vibe with its sliding wood doors and clapping palms that I forgot where I was and fell back onto his platform bed like I was taking a plunge into a spa pool. The moment my back hit the mattress, my eyes got big.

"I don't know what I was thinking," I said. "I'm not ready to sleep with you yet."

"No worries," he replied, falling down next to me. "I'm not ready to sleep with you either."

His words were so reassuring that I didn't try to stop the ensuing kiss or his roaming hand down my backside. Instead, I just enjoyed the moment his hand reached my derriere.

"Mmm. Good butt," he said. "I'm a butt guy, FYI." Being the girl who wrapped a towel around my butt every time I got up from a lounge chair to walk to the pool while donning a bikini, his compliment felt great. "Shall we continue the tour?" he asked.

I liked that he knew when to stop groping and told him I'd love to see the rest of his house. Walking across the hall, Richard opened the door to a second bedroom. Clothes were strewn on the floor and the bed wasn't made. "This is my brother's room," he said apologetically. "I asked him to move out because he's really messy."

It seemed a little harsh to kick one's own brother out over an unmade bed, but I didn't have much time to dwell on it. Richard was already down the hall, opening a third door. "This is my best friend Mike's room," he said. "Mike and I used to practice law together when I was an entertainment lawyer."

Although I was surprised Richard had a second roommate, at the same time it was kind of a relief. Suddenly, Richard's lifestyle seemed a little more relatable. Mike was sitting on the bed, watching T.V. in his workout shorts. He looked younger than Richard, around my age, and hopped out of his bed to greet me. He seemed really affable, like the kind of guy anyone would want to have around. We all chatted a while. Then Richard showed me the gym across the hall before taking me downstairs to the screening room, which was perched right above the tennis court. But for the mahogany paneled walls, it looked like a roller skating rink with its concrete floors. "This will be phase two of construction," Richard said, before informing me he had bought the house a few years ago. "It was like a bad Taco Bell," he said. "I redesigned everything."

Designer. Lawyer. Agent. Landlord. Was there anything this guy didn't do? I wondered as we made our way back upstairs that day and said goodbye.

The following day, I arrived at Playhouse West. Raymond was already there, standing in the corner, punching at the wall like it was a person, emotionally preparing for our scene from *The Days Between*. Raymond was the Denzel Washington of our group, and it was our first time working together since I enrolled here two years ago.

"We're up first," he said, quickly breaking out of character. Playhouse, an ongoing acting conservatory, is based on Sandy Meisner's teachings to create real and truthful behavior by drumming up imaginary circumstances.

I put down my backpack and headed to the bathroom, where God-only-knows how many actors relieved their bowels on a daily basis before putting up a scene for our acting teacher, Robert Carnegie. My stomach was in knots. There were only twelve people in my class, including Scott Caan and James Franco. I couldn't afford to flub this one. The work being done by my peers was so good. Although I was nailing my improvisations, my scene work had fallen under criticism over the last couple months.

The Days Between was about a writing professor who sinks into a deep depression when his student writes a bestseller, the one he never could. Raymond was playing the professor, and I was playing his wife. We'd rehearsed the scene ad nauseum. I was afraid I had no more emotion left to give. I walked to the other dark corner backstage and began drumming up imaginary circumstances that would upset me: *What if I had a little boy and accidentally vacuumed up his gerbil and best friend? What if my dad was allergic to nuts and I accidentally put peanuts in his birthday cupcakes and he died?* It could get kind of morbid. The key was to let one of these dark storylines resonate with you onstage, so you could then transfer the emotions they invoked to your scene.

Raymond and I made our way to the center of the stage without speaking and took seats opposite each other at a small table. He delivered the first line. The heat of his breath on my face triggered a feeling of such intense anger, I stood up and looked at him for several seconds. I hadn't planned this reaction, but the playwright's words were so readily available on my tongue (from all our rehearsing) that they became inconsequential and the behavior took over. Until I was performing my final monologue, at which point I walked across the stage and slithered down the wall in tears. I honestly forgot I was even doing a scene until I heard Robert's voice waft over.

"Bravo," he said. "You just looked like a professional actor."

"Are you sure I didn't run through the middle too quickly?" I asked.

I heard Robert take an annoyed breath. "Just keep up the good work."

I knew not to say anything more and walked to the back of the classroom without looking at anyone. Imaginary circumstance or not, I was emotionally drained and felt really vulnerable after my breakdown. A couple minutes later, I felt a tap on my shoulder and turned around.

"We should work together soon," James Franco whispered.

I was in shock. The only thing we'd ever done on stage together was a word repetition exercise on the day I started, two years earlier. I knew the second we sat opposite each other that he was going to be a star. He looked just like James Dean and was ten years my junior.

On my way home from class, Richard called to see how my day was going. I told him about James and went on and on about my scene and what a breakthrough it had been for me. When I was finally finished, he said, "James Franco is in your class?" I was hurt that he was more focused on James than me but decided to let it go. After all, James was on everyone's radar in Hollywood, and Richard only worked with writers and directors.

When I first moved to L.A., I registered with a casting director to work as an extra to pay my bills. The job comes with the hope that you might be upgraded to a principal: the lead actor whose face is seen.

(Extras, no matter how close they are to the camera, always miss getting into the shot in a way that would make them recognizable to family, friends, or old classmates from high school who might just be wondering what they're up to until seeing them in that Mountain Dew commercial.)

The day after my Academy Award-winning performance, I got called in for a Pantene commercial as a stand-in—a big step up from being an extra. Out of all the pretty girls in the casting director's book, the ad agency had picked me. My call time was five o'clock sharp the following morning. When I arrived to the set, located at a park district pool twenty miles outside of L.A., some guy immediately escorted me to the community center with a sense of urgency that made me think "special treatment." I assumed I was going into hair and makeup. Then a young production assistant with a headset attached to his ear tossed me a wetsuit.

"Here, put this on," he said.

"Where's the dressing room?" I asked.

"Just change behind the wardrobe rack," he said, walking off.

Sidestepping my way around a stack of scaffolding piled in the center of the room and behind the wardrobe rack, I slipped off my clothes. This was definitely not the Marilyn career I had envisioned, I thought, as I slid into the wetsuit (which felt like a suction cup against my skin) and waddled like a penguin out to the pool. Despite still being dark out, it looked like midday. The pool was illuminated with every production light known to man: hair lights, backlights, fill lights, diffusers, and floodlights. Desperate for sunglasses, I brought my hand up to my brow to shield my eyes from the blinding white light. A woman holding a clipboard approached and asked me if I was the stand-in. I told her yes. "Well, go ahead and jump in the pool so we can start lighting the shot," she said.

It was only 5:30 a.m. The principal wasn't due on the set until 7:00. Jumping in at the deep end, I paddled toward the center of the pool. About an hour later, I saw a gorgeous blonde in a terrycloth robe—the principal—nibbling on a croissant under a heat lamp in the distance. My muscles were like jelly from paddling in place for so long, and the skin on my hands was so raw they felt like they were bleeding. As the smell of pancakes began wafting across the water, I didn't think I was going to make it, I was so famished. Then, finally, I heard my new favorite word being yelled in the background by the director. "Breakfast!"

Oh, thank God.

Hoisting my prune-like self out of the water, I headed straight to the craft service truck. "Girl, what happened to that head?" a flamboyant hairstylist asked as he approached. I reached up and touched my locks in that way you touch your earlobes after someone compliments your earrings because you forgot which ones you'd put on. "It's kind of green," he said, pulling a compact out of his fanny pack and holding it up for me to view my reflection. "Chlorine can do that to highlighted hair." My eyes started to well up with tears. "Don't worry. I can fix it," he said, leading me by the hand to his trailer.

I don't know what was worse: the scent of food wafting all around me or my new Grinch-like reflection. But I was so hungry and weak I couldn't say anything, so I just sat down in his chair and let him do his thing. Several minutes later, he spun me around to face the mirror.

"Ta Da!" he said.

"You took off more than seven inches," I said in shock.

"Back from breakfast!" the director yelled in the background. "Where's my stand-in?"

I burst into tears. Again.

"Don't worry. It'll grow," the stylist said, ushering me out of his trailer.

Remarkably, none of the production crew seemed to notice my striking color or style change when they asked me to jump back into the pool.

The following morning, I went to Umberto's Salon for a fix-it cut and color. It took four hours and, ironically, cost as much as I'd made the day before. I needed a drink. So after I paid for my services, I walked out of the salon and headed up to Nic's Martini Bar. About halfway up the block, a woman passing on the sidewalk stopped me.

"Can I have your autograph?" she asked.

"Pardon?" I said with confusion.

Cocking down her head, she peered at me over her sunglasses. "You *are* Meg Ryan, aren't you?"

I was pretty flattered. Meg was the biggest romantic comedy actress at the moment. I was always the first one in line the day one of her movies came out. "Actually, no, I'm not," I answered with a chuckle.

"Sure you're not," she replied, storming off in a rage.

I shook my head in disbelief. *Did that really just happen?* Suddenly, I wanted to get home to check out my new hairdo in the privacy of my own bathroom. I decided to blow off the drink and walked into Starbucks, which was just across the street from Nic's.

"I'll take a double tall latte with extra foam," I said.

"Name?" the guy behind the counter asked.

"Amy," I replied.

"Are you sure it's not Meg?" he winked flirtatiously.

"Oh, come on!" I said.

"What? You look just like her with that haircut."

When Richard picked me up that night, he went on and on about how much he liked my new 'do. "Short hair shows confidence," he said as we pulled up to valet.

If he only knew, I thought, getting out of the car and walking up to the restaurant.

"So, how was the Pantene shoot?" he asked with sincerity.

"Amazing," I replied. "Just incredible."

That Saturday, my friend Bohdi came over to grab dinner. He and I went to college together and had recently reconnected at a party he threw at his house in Manhattan Beach. Bohdi reminded me of a surfer without a surfboard with his moppy blonde hair, mischievous blue eyes, and infectious smile. He always had on a pair of flip-flops and shorts with pockets, which (I'm quite positive) is where he stored his reefer. He was left of center, mellow, and worked in production for the Farrelly Brothers, who wrote and directed *There's Something About Mary.*

After I found out Brett had cheated on me, Bodhi and I had developed a little crush on each other. It was short-lived and ended right before Christmas, but during its tenure Bohdi had given me a small potted narcissus plant, which I still kept on my bathroom sink. Although it was lovely and fragrant, it was one-tenth the size of my arrangement from Richard. When Bohdi knocked on the door, I didn't want him to feel upstaged and—this time around—managed to quickly hide the little card Richard had written me in my silverware drawer before the second knock.

"Coming!" I screamed.

Bohdi looked disheveled from his thirty-minute drive. His Jeep had no doors, roof, or windows.

"You look like you could use a drink," I said as he stepped inside.

"Thanks, but I'm going to smoke," he replied, reaching into his shorts pocket and pulling out a small bag of weed "Want some?"

"I'll stick with the chardonnay."

"Hey, nice flowers," he said as I headed into the kitchen to fetch my wine.

I was not a pot smoker. I had attempted to be. Once. But that was a decade ago. When I walked back into the living room, Bohdi was taking a big toke off his joint.

"It's really mellow," he said through clenched teeth, passing me the cigarette.

I put my wine glass down on the windowsill and looked at him. "Do you promise it will be fine?"

"Yes. It's Woody Weed."

"What's Woody Weed?"

"Woody Harrelson."

Apparently, Bohdi had met Woody through the Farrelly Brothers, who had cast him in *Kingpin*. It was no shock Woody was a smoker. He openly supported causes involving the rainforest, wore hemp clothing, and was a vegan. I decided his weed must be okay and stretched out my arm. Bohdi passed me the joint. I took a very small inhale. And I mean, world-record small. Then, thirty seconds later, I fell to my knees. My heart was pounding out of my chest and the room was spinning. Bohdi squatted down to my level on the floor.

"Amy, are you okay?" he asked, all worried.

"No! Call an ambulance. I think I'm having a heart attack."

Bohdi put his hands under my armpits and lifted me up to a standing position. "It's okay," he said reassuringly. "It's going to be okay."

"No, it isn't. Feel my heart," I said, placing his hand on my chest. Bohdi's face turned white.

"It is beating awfully fast," he replied. "Maybe we should go get some air."

When we entered the courtyard, my knees buckled, and my legs went numb. I started sobbing. "Can we go back upstairs? I think I need to lie down."

"Sure," Bohdi said as he laced (no pun intended) his arm through mine and patiently walked me to my bedroom. He was really being a saint.

"How's the heart?" he asked fearfully, his face now as white as the narcissus plant he had given me.

"I think it's slowing down a little," I said, sliding into bed, where, over the next several minutes, I fluctuated between tears and hysterical laughter. I felt like a crazy person. Then, ten minutes later, I just went back to feeling normal.

"Want to walk up to Mel's Diner and get something to eat?" I asked. "I'm starving."

Bohdi eyed me suspiciously. "Are you sure you're up for it?"

"Yeah, but that is the last time I will ever smoke that stuff. It never agrees with me."

"I think that's a smart idea," he replied.

"So much for Woody Weed," I said.

A couple of hours later, after Bohdi left, I called Richard to say goodnight. I wanted him to know he was the last man I was thinking about before climbing into bed for the third time that evening. I had declined his invitation early that day for our "one week anniversary date" because I didn't want to break the plans I'd made with Bohdi before Christmas. He told me he was happy I called and asked me how my night was. I told him everything that happened. After I finished my story, there was dead silence. I wondered if I'd shared too much, if Richard was jealous I'd hung out with another guy. Then he chuckled, and I knew I was wrong.

"I know Woody," he said.

That night I went to bed wondering who else Richard knew.

On Monday, Richard's assistant Aaron called and introduced himself. He was charming and affable and said he'd heard all about me and couldn't wait to meet me. He sounded like he was in his early twenties. Then he got down to business and sounded all grown up:

"Richard has a dinner Wednesday night with a new writer he's representing, care to join?"

"There's a birthday party being held at The Whiskey for an executive at Warner Brothers Thursday at seven, can you make it?"

"Matthew Perry's manager is throwing a very private dinner on Friday to celebrate his return from rehab, are you in?"

"Yes."

"Yes."

And… "Most definitely," I replied.

"Great," Aaron said, gleefully. "Richard will call you as soon as he gets out of his meeting." And we hung up.

My head was reeling. *Was this really happening?* I was still just an extra. Although, hopefully not for long. I walked into the bathroom and pulled back my plastic shower curtain, careful not to touch the growing mildew on it. I had to get ready for my callback for *The Bold and the Beautiful* at CBS Studios. As I stepped into the shower, it occurred to me that Richard had just booked me for the next week. Maybe he *had* been a little jealous. This made me giddy.

When I arrived at CBS Studios for my audition later that morning, the other actress there was making dinner plans with the casting director. She had her golden retriever with her, implying that she was definitely like family to these people. Plus, and this is a big one, she looked just like a Victoria's Secret model. I am a thin, all-American-looking blonde with a bubbly personality, blue eyes, and a nice smile. I don't have a perfect body or perfect milky skin, I'm just a girl who was decent enough looking to have done some print work and a few commercials. Just another blonde, as Hollywood always liked to remind me.

After Victoria Secret finished schmoozing, I was able to check in. I noticed on the sign-in sheet that I was first up to audition and headed straight to the waiting room to prepare. When you're reading for "The Producers" of a show, your audition always goes on tape, so how you time yourself to where you need to be emotionally is important. There are no cheating tears for the camera. I sat down, closed my eyes, and found the place I needed to be for my melodrama meltdown. Then, as if on cue, the casting agent walked in with the call sheet.

"Ready, Amy?" she asked.

I hopped out of my chair and grabbed my purse.

"Actually," Victoria Secret said with a slight southern drawl. "Do you all mind if I go first? Betsy has an appointment with the vet at 1:30, and we don't want to be late. Do we Betsy, Betsy, Betsy?" she said, ferociously stroking her golden's ears.

"It's fine with me," the casting director said. "Does that work for you, Amy?"

Bursting at the seams with camera-ready emotions, I hesitated for several seconds. Coming across as anti-animal in a place like L.A. could destroy me. I couldn't come up with a better reason than Betsy why I needed to go first. So I just nodded, sat back down, and closed my eyes. Again.

Twenty minutes later, the casting director came out to get me. I was ushered into a small, dark room with a single camera and a glass wall that I couldn't see beyond but that ten producers could see me through. I turned toward the camera and waited for the little red light to click on. When it did…I had nothing.

Owen lived in a gated Mediterranean in Outpost Estates with his boyfriend, Jesse. The two of them could have been plucked right out of the movie *L.A. Story*, or an Abercrombie ad, or both; they were so quintessentially L.A., with their Prada loafers, tight t-shirts, Greek god biceps, Colgate white teeth, and different ethnicities: Owen, a Caucasian male with a shaved head; and Jesse, an African American with Tracy Chapman hair.

Richard and I were the first guests to arrive, so Jesse gave us a tour of the living room. I felt like I was inside a genie bottle. There were Turkish floor pillows, jewel-colored walls, and Moroccan candelabras. It was the perfect love shack. Tempted to blurt "Who's the master?" I just told them how much I loved all the Middle-Eastern influences everywhere. Then Matthew Perry arrived, and we all headed into the dining room like it was no big deal, but inside I was freaking out. Having grown up watching *Friends*, it turned out he was friends with one of my friends.

As soon as we sat down, a housekeeper made her way around the table with a pitcher of homemade margaritas while Owen fired up a joint. *So this is what a getting-out-of-rehab dinner party looks like in L.A.* I flashed Matthew—who was sitting right across from me but still hadn't looked up from his plate—a sympathetic look. I thought it was insensitive to light up in front of him so soon after recovery. According to the press, the poor guy was struggling with some real demons. Luckily, it didn't seem to faze him. When the joint made its way around the table to Matthew, he turned it—along with the margaritas—down without hesitation. Breathing a quiet sigh of relief (I was always rooting for the underdog, who, I would soon discover, was really just me), Owen held the joint out toward me.

"Amy?"

"Oh, God, no!" I said, a little too emphatically. Matthew looked up at me for the first time and smiled. In fact, all eyes were on me as if, suddenly, I was the interesting one.

"So, what do you do, Amy?" Owen asked as the joint skipped its way past me and went between Richard and Owen for the remainder of its life.

"I'm an actress," I said casually.

"Really! What are you currently working on?"

In such an intimate setting of A-listers, I realized it probably had not occurred to Owen, a manager to many top actors in Hollywood, that the answer to this question could be nothing. So I just gave my best "fake it until you make it" response.

"Currently, I'm just auditioning and studying at Playhouse West several times a week."

"Sounds great," he replied sincerely. I could only assume he thought I was preparing for some demanding role. "Well, what have you been in recently, dear?"

I felt the heat rise to my cheeks. The real answer was "a wetsuit" and I knew "*The Days Between*" wouldn't fly with this crowd. After my flopped audition yesterday, it was clear *The Bold and The Beautiful* was definitely off the table. I was speechless.

"She just did a Pantene commercial," Richard interjected proudly. But the look of pity I got from Owen was just unbearable. I pushed myself away from the table.

"Bathroom?" I asked.

"Upstairs to the left," Owen nodded knowingly.

A couple minutes later, there was a knock on the door before Richard let himself in

"Everything okay?" he asked, scooping me up from behind, all frisky. I don't know if it was the margaritas or weed that blinded him to the humiliation I was feeling, but I realized I was not prepared for how uncomfortable I had felt.

"I want to go home," I said coldly.

Totally taken aback, Richard's body stiffened, but I just couldn't handle this whole *L.A. Story* crowd yet. Or, more specifically, I didn't feel worthy of this *L.A. Story* crowd yet. Everyone was so ahead of me. I thought maybe I needed to catch up with them first. Prove myself. Maybe I needed to find the "living-off-Wonder-bread-peanut-butter-and-jelly-sandwiches" crowd to keep the desire to be an actress burning in my belly before I was too ashamed to own or admit what I was trying to become. Maybe… I had to break things off with Richard.

Then…

The next morning, Richard called me from outside my apartment and asked me to come down. He was sitting in his Mercedes with the top down. Sticking out of the back seat was a framed Indian tapestry.

"This is the piece I thought would look great above your couch," he said grinning. " I have a coffee table sitting in my storage unit as well you could use. It needs a little sanding and stain, but if you want to come take a look at it, I could help you refinish it?"

So after we hung the picture—which transformed my whole apartment into a chic looking pied-a-terre that, for the first time, I really could have imagined a young Marilyn living across the hall from—we went to the hardware store, picked up some supplies, and went back to Richard's house and rolled up our sleeves. He threw on a pair of worn khaki shorts and an old t-shirt, and he gave me an old Oxford. It was like an *I Love Lucy* episode, the two of us sanding and staining and getting messy together. But more than that, the whole thing brought Richard down to earth for me. I saw a real guy who did real-life things. Suddenly, any feelings of being intimidated or overwhelmed by him fell away. I was so touched by his willingness to spend a whole day doing something like this with me. After we set the table in the sun to dry, he stepped toward me and unhooked the buttons on my shirt, and we fell into bed and each other easily.

Come Valentine's Day afternoon, Richard and I were lounging on our backs in his Japanese-style platform bed. The doors were open, and the banana palms were clapping in the breeze.

"I have something for you," he said, reaching under the bed and pulling out a black velvet jewelry box. I sat up in bed and opened it. Inside was a diamond necklace.

"Oh, Richard!" I said, reaching into the box and running my hand across a two-carat solitaire on a platinum chain. "It's beautiful." I felt like Julia Roberts in *Pretty Woman*. Only *my* Richard didn't snap the box shut. Instead, he looked at me with serious eyes.

"I love you," he whispered.

"I love you, too," I said.

A couple of days later, Richard spent the night at my place. When he arrived he seemed distracted and quiet, immediately pulling out scripts he needed to review from his backpack. The insecure part of me wondered if he regretted telling me that he loved me so soon, or if he just hated my place. I sat down next to him on the couch.

"Are you okay?"

"I'm fine," he said dismissively.

I didn't want to make a big deal out of it, so I got up and grabbed a play I was working on in acting class.

"Can I get you something?" I asked.

"I'm fine," he said without looking up.

I pretended to study my lines, but inside I was freaking out. A couple minutes later, I closed my play.

"Are you upset with me?" I asked.

"It has nothing to do with you," he said, putting down his script and looking me in the eyes. "I just had a tough day at work."

That March, I awoke to a phone call from my friend Sloan in New York. Sloan and I went to college together and had stayed in close touch. She worked in marketing for Barneys New York department store, which was no surprise. In college, Sloan was sophisticated beyond her years. While I was sporting a pair of elastic pants from The Limited, she was decked out in Ralph Lauren riding boots and gophers. She was a real character who danced to the beat of her own drum. One Halloween, my sophomore year, she dressed up as a Deadhead—the way she saw them: long flowing skirt, Birkenstocks, and… a tie-dyed t-shirt with all her gold credit cards scotch taped to her chest. Everyone at Boulder knew that half the girls with unshaved legs and dirty dreadlocks had trust funds the size of California. Only Sloan had the nerve to spell it out in a way no else did. Once, I overheard her tell a man she'd been seeing, when he started scratching his privates after they emerged from her bedroom and passed me on the couch without acknowledgment, "You know, there's cream for that sort of thing."

So…

I was surprised when I picked up the phone that morning and she was in tears.

"He told me he couldn't marry me in the cab ride home last night," Sloan said.

"What? There must be some mistake," I said, propping myself up and squinting through the morning light. "Patrick loves you with all his heart. I witnessed it with my own eyes."

I had just stayed with them at their Upper West Side apartment while shooting the small movie role I had booked with Amanda Peet. They seemed happy.

"It's no mistake. I gave him back the ring."

"Oh, Sloan," I said. "What can I do?"

"I want to come out for a visit. I'm thinking a move to Los Angeles might be in the cards."

"Absolutely. Anytime. I think a change of scenery might do you some good."

"My therapist thinks so," she replied, through sniffles. "I will let you know, sweetie."

Three days later, Sloan landed in Los Angeles and picked me up in her rented Mercedes convertible to go to the premiere of *Cruel Intentions*. Richard represented the writer/director of the film and had gotten two tickets for us. "No need to take the Galant," I could almost hear her say when I'd offered to drive.

As we made our way down Sunset, there was a cool breeze in the air and the palm trees glistened pink in the setting sun. In college, Sloan's motto had been, "You can never be too tan, too thin, or too blonde." But as I looked over at her in the driver's seat, now ten years later, I realized this motto had been modified drastically. She was white as a porcelain doll. Sunscreen was lathered on her arms, and a big floppy hat and Jackie O sunglasses protected a fuller but most beautiful face. She looked like she could be the movie star when we pulled up to the theatre—where fans were lined up along the sidewalk screaming the names of their favorite stars and camera bulbs flashed like Christmas tree lights on crack. Winking at Sloan as we got out of the car, I handed a big man guarding the velvet-roped entrance our VIP passes before we made our way down the red carpet to the theatre. Sloan was right where she belonged: Hollyweird.

Richard was waiting for us in the lobby. He looked like a true Hollywood agent in his gray suit, Italian shoes, and Oliver People sunglasses. He acted like one, too. When I introduced him to Sloan, he seemed so disinterested. Thank God Sloan didn't seem to pick up on this. Her gaze was on Selma Blair, the star of the movie, who was just ahead of us.

"Oh, sweetie," Sloan turned and whispered in my ear. "I'm moving here."

Our seats were right behind Selma. Of course, Richard went to law school with Selma's date. He informed us they had just gotten engaged. We all offered our congratulations. Then Selma turned around in her seat and ran her left arm across her fiancé's back the way one of Bob Barker's girls on *The Price is Right* runs her hands across a new refrigerator or car to show off her four-carat ring. *Isn't a movie enough bling for one night?* I thought. I took Richard's hand and squeezed hard. I was bursting with creativity I was dying to put into my own movie role. Only no one was hiring me.

After the premiere, we made our way to the after party at a restaurant across the street from the theatre. Within ten minutes, I saw Sloan flirting with one of the guys in the film. Richard and I made our way to an empty couch in the far corner of the room and sat down. It was the first time we'd been alone together all night. He put his arm around me and looked into my eyes.

"I want you to move in," he said.

Moving into Richard's house coincided nicely with moving into a new decade. I was turning thirty in less than a week, so Richard offered to host a birthday dinner and cook for all my girlfriends. When I said Richard was very "metro," I wasn't kidding. Besides decorating and design, his other passion was cooking. Watching him chop an onion or cut a tomato was like watching Julia Child. I felt like the luckiest girl in the world when I handed Richard my guest list for the party.

My best girlfriends at the time were Sloan, Annie, Polly, Lila, Liz, and Kat. I went to college with Sloan, Annie, and Kat; and I'd met, Polly, Lila, and Liz when I moved to L.A. two years before. Liz, Polly, and Annie were all pursuing acting like me. Annie was the comedian of our group and did stand-up around town; Polly was the actress-turned-writer; and Liz and I were in acting class together. Lila was a bathing suit designer and former super-model whom you never wanted to get caught dead next to in a bikini; and Kat was a successful food and fashion photographer for *Martha Stewart*, *Vogue*, and *Elle*. All my girls were kind, hardworking people. Even uber successful Richard had said, when he offered to cook for them, "You know, I never really wanted to hang out with any of my exes' friends, but I really like yours."

A couple days before my birthday, Richard and I were taking a scenic drive down Mulholland and stopped to take in the view. We got out of the car at this vista overlooking the valley. Universal Studios was in the distance, which got me all freaked out because I was on the eve of my thirtieth birthday and all the acting roles—at this point in time—were going to teenagers, which is not always the case. The type of movies and television shows being produced is cyclic. One year, the films being made may call for twenty-five-year-old actors; another year, it could be forty-year-old actresses. But it was 1999, a.k.a., the year of the teenager in Hollywood.

"I can't believe I'm going to be thirty," I said, leaning back into Richard, who had his arms around me. "I feel scared."

"I understand," he replied. "It's nearly impossible to make it as an actress after thirty."

I went numb as a wave of insecurity filled my head like a flock of birds descending on breadcrumbs. I wanted to believe that Richard was just trying to protect me. Just like an ER doc, he knew the worse case scenarios of Hollywood, which were if you are over twenty-five trying to be an actress and your mom isn't Goldie Hawn, get out. Still, I felt unsupported. Yes, we all knew the odds were against me making it in Hollywood, but plenty of people did make it. And Richard and I knew many of them. I needed to hold out for a little longer.

The day before my birthday, my mom flew out to meet Richard and see my new living quarters. I couldn't wait for them to meet. After I picked her up at the airport, we headed straight to meet Richard for lunch. When we arrived at the restaurant, Richard was already sitting at a corner table with a menu. I excitedly rushed up and introduced them to each other.

"I've heard so much about you from Amy. It's great to finally be here and meet," my mom said as she sat down.

"Likewise," Richard said, and he brought the menu up to his face and didn't say much more for the remainder of lunch, unless my mom asked him direct questions. I felt really awkward and wondered if Richard was intimidated. My mom was young compared to most of my friends' moms and very easy on the eyes, a cross between Olivia Newton-John and Donna Mills. Growing up, all the boys in my class had a crush on her. She was definitely the M.I.L.F. of my school. But Richard worked in Hollywood, I thought. He interacted with pretty women every day. Plus, despite my mom's good looks, she never gave off that Mrs. Robinson vibe and was the easiest person in the world to talk to—so much so, in fact, that some of my high school friends, who don't even stay in touch with me, still call her to catch up. Maybe Richard just didn't like my mom, I thought, as he kissed me goodbye after lunch and told us he'd see us back at the house.

When my mom and I got in the car, I apologized for Richard's quietness and said he wasn't usually like that. She told me not to be silly, that he was probably just in work mode. It was so like my mom to deflect any negativity and keep it positive. In fact, I was surprised she didn't suggest I "have an iced tea and go take a nap," her usual reply when things got a bit uncomfortable.

The next night, Richard was a warm, charitable host. He refilled wine glasses when they were empty, sang "Happy Birthday" to me while carrying the cake, and twirled, dipped, and kissed me after I blew out my candles and made my wish: *I want to be a working actress.*

For every one guest I'd invited to my birthday, Richard invited fifty to his—for a grand total of one thousand people. The night required a doorman and a bodyguard. Each of them was given strict instructions from Richard: "No one gets in that's not on the list!" *But how many more could there be?* I wondered, as I stood on Richard's balcony and took in the sea of strangers below me. It was like a Coachella concert down there. There was no one in Hollywood left.

One of the guests who showed up was my ex-boyfriend, Brett. He came as someone's "plus one."

"Did you read my letter?" he asked when we bumped into each other in the screening room. It was an awkward moment. I had never responded to his nine-page confession about why he hadn't called me over Christmas break. Even though he had a very good explanation (he went on a sailing trip with his family and had no cell phone reception at sea), Richard had already swooped in and intrigued me; and he had already cheated. Still, I was surprised by the twinge of excitement fluttering in my belly when I saw him and told him that I hoped we could be friends and gave him a kiss on the cheek.

"So you really live here?" he asked with a chuckle.

"I know," I said, shrugging. "It's hard to believe that just six months ago we were making out in my run-down apartment."

"Totally," he replied.

Later in the evening, I was in my bedroom, trying to manage ten women who had found their way into my closet. They wanted to take a Jacuzzi and were looking for bathing suits. Luckily, my good friend Lila, the swimwear designer, had gifted me with every string bikini she'd ever designed. Passing them out like candy, I was the most popular girl at the party. Was this really my life?

Then the next day came, and with it: four thousand empty beer bottles and cigarette butts to clean up. I even found a line of coke on a mirror under the guest bathroom vanity, which I immediately flushed down the toilet. "Never again," I said to Richard, who just shrugged off the news like I was telling him the toilet was clogged. But I felt violated in some way. I did not like all the stranger dangers going on in my house.

That June, Bohdi called. "I hooked you up with an audition for the Farrelly Brothers' next movie, *Me, Myself, and Irene*," he said. "Jim Carrey's already slated to star. You'll be reading for the part of the hotel manager. I'll overnight you the script. And…"

"Yeah?"

"Don't fuck it up," he replied with a chuckle.

But I knew he wasn't kidding and promised him I wouldn't. Bohdi had hooked me up once before for an audition with them when I had just moved to L.A., in a movie they wrote called *There's Something About Mary*. I'd gotten dumped by my San Francisco boyfriend the night before and really botched it up. I could still hear the Farrellys' words ringing in my head after I finished my dark, lifeless read for them. "You know this is a comedy, right?"

The following day, I was like one of Pavlov's dogs waiting for the script to arrive. Any time I heard anything resembling a bell—telephone, intercom, car horn—I ran to the door salivating. The script finally came around 3:00. Ripping it out of the plastic envelope, I scanned each page with my index finger, looking for the part of "Hotel Manager." When I finally found it, toward the end, I was confused and reread the page: *Hotel Manager is a heavyset, black MAN in his late 40s.*

"But I am a thirty-year-old blonde on the verge of anorexia," I said in despair.

I immediately called Bohdi and asked him if there had been some mistake. He told me there hadn't. "Just think outside the box," he said reassuringly. "And remember… the zanier the better. The Farrellys like unique."

The role only had four lines, but I put some real thought into the character anyway. I decided the hotel manager's backstory should be that of a young woman who'd been waiting years for something dramatic to happen at her podunk hotel—like a murder or robbery. I chose to wear a Sherlock Holmes-type coat and put a fake detective badge inside the inner pocket so I'd be ready to flash it toward the Farrelly Brothers. Then, so they would be sure not to remember me from my last audition, I threw a green mud mask on my face and put my hair up in pink sponge rollers.

I was ready.

When I walked into the waiting room on the day of my audition, I was not so sure I was ready at all. Every actor in there stopped talking and looked up at me like I was, quite simply put, crazy. No one was in costume. Even my best friend Annie, who was also auditioning and was in the waiting room, wouldn't acknowledge me. *Maybe I went too far in committing to this character*, I thought.

"Amy Karl?" a casting director came out and yelled.

"That's me," I said, in this moment feeling bad for my dad that I was his legacy.

"You're up," he said, eyeing me suspiciously.

There were about ten guys in the auditioning room. There would have been eleven, but I begged Bohdi not to come in because I thought his presence would make me too nervous. Thank God he obliged because all the guys stopped talking upon my entrance. "You know YOU are not the comedy, the script is, right?" ran through my head, as I stood there getting a stare-down.

"Whenever you're ready," one of the producers said.

"Okay," I said, before I launched into my lines the way a linebacker goes in for a tackle—with my whole heart. Then I waited as one of the Farrelly Brothers consulted my headshot and whispered something to the others.

"This is you?" he asked, through a chuckle, holding up my headshot.

"Yeah." I said, with as much confidence as I could muster.

"We'd like you to read for a bigger part. Can you stick around?"

I must have been smiling at this point because my facemask pulled so hard against my lips they felt like they were splitting in half.

"I'd love to," I said, and a producer told me which scene I'd be performing and handed me a script before I exited the room.

It turned out the bigger part I was reading for was the part of Jim Carrey's wife in the opening of the movie. I noticed that the role called for "cute," so over the next several minutes I panicked. Except for a peach-colored sweater that washed me out and was reeking of gasoline, I didn't have any flattering clothes in the trunk of my car, like an actress should for just this sort of emergency. Still, it would just have to do, so I ran to the bathroom and quickly changed out of the Sherlock Holmes coat before attempting to wash all the green goo off my face.

Unfortunately, the only soap available to me was in a dispenser and the only towel to dry my face with was the brown paper towel that also comes out of a dispenser and feels like sandpaper. My cheeks looked like one big red pimple after scrubbing off the mask, and I didn't think to bring any makeup concealer with me because I came in a green mask. So I just stopped looking in the mirror so I wouldn't get psyched out, went back outside, and started to run my lines out loud on the sidewalk.

"Want some help?" a young man who looked like Tom Cruise and was also waiting to audition asked.

I had absolutely no idea who this guy was, but I knew I needed all the help I could get.

"Sure," I said, proceeding to run my lines with him.

"I think you should play the character much stronger and tougher than that," he said when I finished.

I had nothing to lose with two minutes to prepare, so I took his suggestion and tried it again before the casting director came out to tell me they were ready to see me. My eyes were twitching when I walked back into the room. I dug my fingernails into my palms for grounding.

"Any questions?" one of the producers asked me. I said no.

"Whenever you're ready."

I took a deep breath that connected me to the earth and launched into the scene. And when I finished, something truly miraculous happened: I got a standing ovation from the ten men in front of me.

"Bravo," one man yelled. And, "This is how I imagined the words would look," another man said.

I don't think I had allowed anything in my life to ever feel this good.

Every Saturday, Richard hosted a basketball game from 10:00 to noon for a bunch of guys on our tennis court. It was like the "who's who" of Hollywood out there. The game often included the likes of Woody Harrelson, Will Farrell, Dean Cain, and several Hollywood producers. I never got a chance to talk to them because they didn't come through the house to get to the tennis court. They took the outside stairs next to the garage.

The Saturday following my audition, I was in the kitchen making a smoothie when Richard walked in, drenched in sweat.

"Brad told me you gave the best read," he said.

I immediately turned off the blender and looked at Richard. Brad played basketball at the house and, I had just found out that week, was one of the producers on *Me, Myself, and Irene.*

"Do you think I got the part?" I asked.

"I don't know," he said. "But he said you were a good actress."

A few days later, I was on the bed leafing through a magazine with a grin on my face. Still riding the high of my audition, I was feeling confident I might get the role (as an actress you don't know if you'll get news about booking the day of the audition, two weeks later, a month later, or never) when Richard walked in after work.

"I spoke to Brad today," he said. "They offered the part to Denise Richards. Apparently, she draws ten million at the box office, which I was really surprised by. But who knows if she'll even be available."

"You mean she might not take it?"

"Maybe," he said.

"Must be nice," I replied, my shoulders drooping.

"While we're on the topic of box office draw, do you think you could invite James Franco to our next party or talk to him? WMA is really interested in signing him."

I was totally taken aback by Richard's timing and felt slighted.

"Maybe," I said, in the same jealous tone I'd had with James the first time I sat across from him in acting class.

"Our talent department signed a new actress today off her tape," he continued. "I think she's going to be a star."

"Really," I replied.

"Yeah. Her tape was amazing. She just walked into frame and did nothing but say, 'Piper Perabo.' It was so intriguing."

I wanted to slit my wrists.

Two weeks later, I walked down to the screening room to get something out of the bathroom, which was through this secret paneled door and really hard to find. It was a Saturday morning, and I could see all the guys playing basketball outside because the screening room sat right above the tennis court. But today, I took no interest in what bigwig was playing. I had spent the last two weeks walking around like I'd been lobotomized, and no matter how much I willed myself to snap out of it, I couldn't. I think the rejection of two years of acting was catching up with me.

Then...

Woody Harrelson walked into the room, and my mind started SPINNING. He was the Farrelly Brothers' golden boy, the King Pin. Rumor had it that Denise Richards still hadn't accepted the role. Perhaps he could put in a good word for me. Crazier things had happened, I thought, as I watched Woody look around the room like a lost little puppy with his fanny pack.

"Let me guess," I said, turning the corner around the stairs. "Bathroom?"

"Yeah," he replied with a smile. "Do you know where it is?"

"Only when I'm sober, and I live here," I answered, feeling the wall for the door.

"I'm Woody," he said.

"Oh, I know who you are," I replied in a playful tone. "Your weed almost killed me."

An amused look spread across his face. I knew it was time to turn on the charm. I told him all about the night with Bohdi and how I'd auditioned for the role they offered Denise, making sure to add, "if…she was available." When I was finally finished, Woody just looked at me. I thought he was on the brink of offering some inspiring story or actorly advice when, suddenly, he reached inside his fanny pack and pulled out a baggy.

"Can I offer you some trail mix?" he said with a big smile. "It's all vegan."

In this moment, it was pretty clear this was all the love I was going to get from Woody or anyone else on this movie for that matter. And—to add salt to the wound—the following week I found out that Denise didn't take the part, so they offered it to the lead actress on *Two Guys, a Girl and a Pizza Place.*

One night in early July, Sloan and I were sipping on glasses of wine and enjoying the people watching from a sidewalk café on Sunset Plaza. It was an excruciatingly slow month for auditioning, and Sloan was taking the summer to enjoy L.A. and recuperate from her broken engagement before looking for a "real" job. She'd worked her butt off in New York so she could afford the hiatus. As the fifth Ferrari of the evening pulled up with another man in his late fifties, wearing gold chains, Sloan looked over at me.

"I think we should take a stab at writing a screenplay," she said.

"About what?" I laughed.

"I think it should be the female version of *Swingers* but with a more spiritual slant." *Swingers* had been all the rage the year before: an independent film written and directed by its lead actor who was sick of waiting for the studio system to approve of him. So instead, he'd created his own breakout vehicle.

"Sure, we can call it *Gallo and God*," I said, raising my wine glass in jest.

"Actually…that's kind of brilliant," Sloan replied, deep in thought. "Richard can represent us and we will be on our way."

Seeing how my career was playing out just like *Swingers'* main character, I suspected this idea could probably write itself. I accepted Sloan's invitation.

"To Gallo and God," I said, raising my glass.

"To Gallo and God!" Sloan returned the toast.

Sloan and I had never written a script. Yet, somehow, by the end of that bottle of wine we knew we must write ours in two weeks or less. We also knew that, to accomplish this goal, we couldn't be distracted. Sloan suggested we road trip to her parents' new home in Vail and write there. Apparently, it was some sprawling estate of tranquility nestled in the mountains, on a creek. Sloan promised there would be "no distractions" and suggested we drive out that week. I told her it would be fun to take the convertible, and she informed me that we would be driving my Galant because her mom had no idea that her dad had bought her a Mercedes convertible and this could really piss off her mom.

Two days later, we were making our way down I17. We had planned to use every minute of the seventeen-hour road trip to flush out our plot before writing, but two hours into our road trip, Sloan pointed toward a young blonde girl on the side of the road.

"Look, there's a hitchhiker," she said.

I asked Sloan if I should pull over and pick her up.

"Absolutely," she replied. "She's too young and pretty to be hitching."

The girl told us she ran out of gas. She was in tears and out of money and needed to call her dad. We drove her to the nearest gas station, paid for her phone call, and waited with her until her dad got there. Three hours later, we were back on the road, singing along to the Grateful Dead. Five miles from her parents' exit in Vail, Sloan turned off the radio.

"Maybe we should talk about the plot now," she said.

I tightened my grip on the steering wheel and went into thinking mode for several seconds. "I got it! Why don't we study *Swingers* scene by scene and see how we can rewrite those scenes using girls. After all, everything's 'a derivative.'"

"Perfect" she said.

Ready to begin our writing adventure, I drove down her parents' long driveway and looked around in confusion. "What's this?" I asked.

"What?"

"The moving trucks," I said.

Sloan had failed to mention that her parents were just moving into their home in Vail. And I don't mean "just last week" or "just last night." I mean just as we arrived. Over a dozen men were outside hauling boxes, fighting over the best way to hang the chandelier, one that Vince Vaughn's character in *Swingers* might have described as "money" because it was so massive.

"Sorry," Sloan squealed as we stepped into the foyer, where her mom was delegating tasks.

"China?" a moving man asked as Sloan rushed off, leaving her mom no alternative but to turn to me and ask if I would be so kind as to take the next box into the kitchen. And this was how it went for the next six hours and forty boxes. Until, finally, the sun was setting, and I could almost taste a glass of wine in my future. Instead, I heard Sloan's desperate plea for help. I got to her first and saw that her leg had been pinned underneath her dad's thousand-pound pool table. She was in tears, explaining how she had hung her .001-pound sweater on one of the pool table legs propped against the wall when we arrived, and how when she pulled it off a few moments ago, it had caused the pieces to fall on top her like a set of dominoes.

It took a crew of workers to pry the disassembled pieces off Sloan's leg, which appeared not to be broken, just badly bruised. To be sure, though, her dad called 911 for an ambulance. "I forgot to renew my insurance policy" and "I'm so bummed I can't do aerobics this week" was all Sloan could muster as we carried her outside to the driveway. Curled up on the asphalt, cradling her bruised leg as we waited for the ambulance to arrive, it seemed Sloan was about to go into shock, she was shaking so badly. A helpful worker rushed back with a blanket. "Not the cashmere," her mom said, calm, cool, and collected from the front step, as her dad swore obscenities a sentence long before placing a cardboard box over Sloan to protect her from the rain that had started to come down.

I could tell her parents were no strangers to the drama. And God only knows, neither was I. Needless to say, we got off to a slow start writing in Vail. Then, when Sloan's bruised leg was better, John F. Kennedy Jr.'s plane went down and we were glued to the television for two days. We were all devastated by the news. Still, Sloan and I persevered those last five days in Vail, writing fifteen hours a day, then another ten the week we got back home. Finally, we had a completed first draft we were both really proud of.

The afternoon the screenplay was done, I went to a barbeque with Richard. I was chatting with some big executive who told me he produced small movies.

"Well, I just wrote the next must-see independent," I told him.

"Love the confidence," he chuckled. "What's it about?"

"Think *Swingers* meets Deepak Chopra."

"Wow! Sounds interesting. I'd love to read it," he said, passing me his card.

By the time we got home, Richard was chomping at the bit to read the script. He had heard the whole exchange between the executive and me. It felt good to have Richard take such a huge interest and helped squash any feelings I'd had of him not being supportive of my career in Hollywood. As I passed him my script and watched him walk into his office and close the door, I was confident I had my breakout vehicle.

Later that evening, I stood behind the door listening for laughs. After three hours, I couldn't take it anymore and walked into the room. Richard was lying on the couch, which was across from the desk, snoring with the script splayed across his chest. There was a "B-" circled in red on the cover page that he had obviously written. I was devastated and tiptoed out of the room.

The next day, I couldn't get out of bed. Richard asked me what was wrong. I told him I was discouraged, that I thought he'd like my script more.

"What makes you so special?' he said with a blank stare.

I knew Richard wasn't trying to be harsh. Rather, he was trying to take the pressure off me and impart wisdom: *Everyone would love to write a masterpiece right out of the gate—but who could? Not too many. So why should you?* Still, it's never just what you say; it's how you say it. Where was that loving guy who'd helped me on the tennis court? Where was I? I understood that dating an actress was not the easiest thing in the world, especially when she wasn't in a Zen place with her craft. Just like that day on the tennis court with Richard, now many moons ago, I wanted my script to be like my winning cross-court shot that made me feel like I was back on my game. I wanted Richard to help me achieve that winning feeling.

I looked like someone being weaned off heroine in rehab: body shaking uncontrollably, sweating like a pig, drooling on my yoga mat from concentrating so hard on not falling out of triangle pose, a.k.a., downward facing dog.

"You poor thing," Sharika said, as she walked up and pushed down on my hip bones, causing me to convulse a little more. "You're a mess." I couldn't believe my ears and dropped down to my knees in defeat. Weren't yoga teachers supposed to be non-judgmental and positive about everything? "Up, up, up, up," she continued. "Let's get this shit aligned."

Apparently, she was a different kind of yoga instructor. I popped my buttocks back into the air as Sharika pressed down on my lower vertebrae. "This is your first chakra," she continued. "It stores your stresses relating to work, home, finance, relationship, and a need to feel like you belong. If you feel insecure in any of these areas, this pose will help you take root," she said, before instructing the class into its next pose.

"Lightly walk or jump your feet up. *Uttanasana!*"

It's true. I was a mess.

When a standing ovation at an audition, a bump-in with Woody, a friendship with Bohdi, a boyfriend at a top agency, and a B- screenplay still wasn't enough to land me a part, I knew it was time to expand beyond acting. While the days in Richard's calendar remained busy, predictable, and sexy, lately, the only thing written on a day in my calendar was 'take a shower' or 'pick up toilet paper.' It was getting pathetic.

One night at the end of July, I was on the bed listlessly leafing through a magazine. Any hope or excitement that I might book a part any time soon was gone. Richard walked into the room.

"Maybe it's time to get my real estate license," I blurted. I'd sold real estate back in Chicago for a couple of years after graduating from college and before moving to California to pursue an acting career. I'd done fairly well in the business and was even the recipient of "The Young Up And Coming Sales Associate of The Year Award" from my company.

Richard approached the foot of the bed. "If you could just make fifty thousand a year, I would be good with that," he said.

I found this comment so annoying, considering I moved to L.A. to be an A-list actor like all the A-list actors who were coming through the doors of the house I now lived in. Instead, I was a struggling actress who didn't have two dimes to rub together and was starting to feel like a phony living in this house that had a bigger identity than I did—a house that made others assume I was the kind of person who should have no problems and lived a life of bliss. Because in a way, like me, the house was an archetype, something that screamed to the outside world that if you lived behind the gates of a place like this than it meant you had "arrived" and should be happy and never complain or be ungrateful.

"I think I'll strive for a little better than that," I said.

"That's fine. If you get your license, I'll give you the listing on this house when I'm ready to sell."

Although I was deeply touched by this overture, it was all I could do not to tell him how that should cover the fifty thousand dollars he'd be good with me making because that's how much my commission on a house of this caliber would be. The whole thing was a little condescending. But I knew I was on the defense and just told him how much his vote of confidence meant.

The next day I drove out to Santa Monica and signed up with the real estate school and picked up my books.

The last Saturday in July, Richard and I sponsored a celebrity basketball tournament at the house to benefit the Best Buddies Foundation. Best Buddies is a charity started by the Shriver family to support kids with developmental disabilities. E! Entertainment was slated to cover the event, and all the guys who played basketball at the house were lined up to play in the tournament. I was on the organizing committee and so was Sloan.

The day of the event, there were over 1,500 people in attendance, including Richard's whole agency, which gave them a lot of good press. Everyone was swimming, eating, drinking, and watching basketball. I was proud to be a part of such a meaningful day, but it was a lot of work and, like all the parties Richard threw, I'm sure…expensive.

Two hours into the party, Richard and I stole our first private moment together by the pool. I wanted to let him know how much I appreciated his charitable heart.

"You know, it was really nice of you to sponsor and support such a great event. I'm sure it wasn't cheap," I said.

"I didn't pay for anything," he responded flatly. "Red Bull did. In fact, I always try to get a sponsor for all my parties." Suddenly, it all made sense.

"Of course," I said nonchalantly. "Nevertheless, I hope everyone appreciates you. It was kind of you to open the house."

A few minutes later, I walked into our master bathroom to catch my breath. We had a "do not enter" sign taped to the door so guests would use the bathroom down the hall. So I was surprised when I turned the corner and saw a little girl taking a bubble bath in my tub.

"Well, hello. Who are you?" I asked in a surprised but friendly tone.

"Now, come on, get out of there, honey. Who knows what crap is in that soap," a familiar-sounding man's voice wafted from behind.

I turned around and saw Woody Harrelson—the vegan.

"Oh, hi," I said.

"Hey," he replied indifferently as he picked (I assumed) his daughter up out of the tub. It was clear he didn't remember me. For the first time, I was relieved I was getting my real estate license. I needed a break from these people.

Over the next two weeks, all I did was study for my real estate exam. Richard had a great office off the living room, with a little balcony that opened out to a view. Every morning, I would go in the office, lock the door, and not come out until I had read one chapter and taken the quiz at the end of it. Although it was pretty boring stuff compared to the Farrelly Brothers and green face masks, it was a relief to use my left brain and have something tangible in my hand at the end of each day, like a quiz with an "A" on it. Society's perception of success is about a person who looks good on paper. I couldn't prove to anyone on a page that my stage work in Monday's acting class had been brilliant.

When I finished taking the exam in August, the woman monitoring the classroom handed me a piece of paper with a phone number on it. She told me to call the hotline in two weeks for my results.

When I finally got word, Richard was in the guest bedroom taking a nap. I slithered under the covers and spooned him from behind.

"I passed the test," I whispered into his ear.

He turned over and stroked my head gently. "I'm so proud of you," he said with a smile. I felt like it was a fresh start for us. Like I should put acting behind me.

A week later, I got a call from a theatrical agent I'd sent a mission statement to back when I was dating Brett. It stated all the reasons why he should represent me. He asked if I could come down to his talent agency that week. Two days later, I was sitting across from him in his very impressive office with Herman Miller chairs, Persian rugs, and an original Andy Warhol hanging on his wall.

"So, what do you do outside of acting?" he asked nonchalantly, consulting my headshot and resume from behind his glass desk without looking up at me.

Other than my small movie role, a few commercials, and my stint at the American Conservatory Theatre, my resume was pretty thin. I knew he'd assume I must do other things to fill my time, so I was proud to confirm that now, in fact, I finally did.

"I sell real estate," I replied confidently.

"Well, which one are you going to be, Amy? Actor or Realtor? Because, clearly, Hollywood can't see you as both now, can it?"

"I don't know...I just read that Kevin Costner sold insurance in between his auditions."

"Well, he's Kevin Costner," the agent snapped before informing me that his next appointment was waiting and his secretary would see me out.

I wanted to scream but gathered my things without saying another word and headed straight to AGO, my favorite restaurant. Ironically, Richard had made a dinner reservation there earlier that week to celebrate me getting my real estate license. When I arrived, he was already at the bar, waiting for our table. I walked over and pulled out the stool next to him.

"Amy?" a woman's voice wafted. I turned around and saw an acquaintance from college I hadn't seen in years. We exchanged hugs. I introduced her to Richard. "So, what have you been doing with your life?" she asked.

I thought being able to say, "I'm a Realtor," would be a huge relief. But it wasn't. My heart sank when I told her I was going to start selling real estate. So I opened up about how I'd been pursuing acting for the past several years.

Later that night, while Richard and I were waiting for our cars in valet, he turned toward me. "You should just say you sell real estate because, technically, that's what you do."

"What if I'm in an acting meeting?" I asked, beyond frustrated.

"Then just wear the acting hat. But never wear two hats at once. Otherwise, people won't take you seriously."

I decided Richard was right. Being a Realtor when I was out socially and selling real estate and just an actor when I was on an audition would be my new rule.

Two weeks before Thanksgiving, Richard wanted to "test" the market. So I listed the house for 3.4 million. The first person to look at it was a guy by the name of Darren Starr. I didn't know who Darren Starr was. What I did know was that his Realtor, Sharona, was the "it" real estate agent in Hollywood. Richard had known her for years and told me she was the woman I should try to emulate because she represented the who's who in town. He also told me she was the girl about whom the song "My Sharona" was written (I'm not kidding).

The day of the showing, I expected a snobby, intimidating professional in an Armani suit to show up at my door. Instead, a very down-to-earth woman in jeans and a t-shirt greeted me. She had a very Valley Girl, perhaps-we-could-roll-a-joint-later vibe about her, and her client Darren Starr was just your average-looking guy in an Izod shirt and Adidas tennis shoes. Still, I was determined to play the role of consummate real estate professional.

"Shall we start in the kitchen?" I asked, all serious.

Sharona shrugged.

"As you can see, no details were spared. The appliances are all Viking, and the door hinges came from Prague, offering unparalleled architectural integrity," I said, as if these words were part of my everyday vocabulary.

"Excuse me," Darren interrupted, as I gushed over some tile Richard had imported from Italy. "Has anyone ever told you, you look like (*Here it comes*, I thought) Elizabeth Shue?"

Even though it was so refreshing to hear that I resembled someone other than Meg, I wasn't about to mix door hinges and actors today. I decided not to get into it.

"No," I replied.

"Well, are you an actress?" he asked pointedly.

One hat, one hat, one hat.

"Me? Oh, no, I'm just a real estate agent," I answered.

A few moments later, Sharona and I were down in the screening room waiting for Darren to finish using the bathroom. I was leaning against the couch, and Sharona was facing me when we made eye contact.

"Do you know who my buyer is?" Sharona mouthed dramatically.

"No," I mouthed back.

"It's Darren Starr."

"Who's that?" I asked before he emerged from the bathroom.

"You know, the creator of *Sex and the City.* He's always looking to cast people. Aren't you also an actress?" she asked, confused.

No, I am a self-sabotaging moron who plays by everyone else's rules. An idiot who's beyond recovery, I thought as Darren emerged from the bathroom and informed Sharona that he was ready to move on to the next house. This one just wasn't for him.

"Good luck with the sale," he said, having lost all interest in me, and quickly exiting out the side door.

I tried to find the words, "Wait! Don't go! Everyone tells me I look like Elizabeth Shue! And,

yes, I really am an actress who adores your show!"
But there was just no time. He was already gone.

After a couple more showings with no offers, Richard
decided to take the house off the market until Phase
3 of construction was done and the holidays were
over. Sloan invited us to spend New Year's at her
parents' home in Vail. We were going to be in Aspen
for Christmas, so it was perfect. I told her we'd love
to come ring in the new millennium with her.

"Good," she said. "But I want to warn you in
advance that I won't be skiing, snowboarding, or waking up early to make you breakfast. So you will have
to make yourself at home." I assured her that was fine.

On our first night in Vail, I wondered if Richard
took Sloan's comment a little too literally. To me
"making yourself at home" meant helping yourself to
a glass of water without asking or clearing the plates
from the table without being summoned. But taking over the kitchen to prepare a three-course meal
that required chopping, grilling, sautéing, roasting,
baking, and use of the family Cuisinart the minute
Sloan's parents went to dinner? This meant something else completely: Arrogance, perhaps?

Draining my third glass of wine, I watched
Richard stir the au poivre. "Where on earth is Sloan?"
I slurred. But I knew exactly where she was: still in
bed with her new, hot, ten-years-younger, trying-
to-be-a-musician lover, staying all-too-true to her
promise about not playing host.

"Sloan!" I yelled at the top of my lungs. "We're about to serve dinner!"

"Oh, Amy," Richard said in a disapproving tone. "Just chop the salad."

"Fine," I replied, as I grabbed a cutting board and sliced tomatoes. "But I'm not okay with this."

"It's fine," he said, like some holier-than-thou spiritual guru who thinks they're more evolved than you are. But it wasn't fine. Richard had been distant all week. He'd left me on the slopes to fend for myself. Hadn't helped me get my skis. And had pretty much spent the last hour cooking in silence. Where had my guy from the tennis court gone?

"Here," he said, as I reached for my second tomato. "Let me show you a better way to cut that."

I was about to ask him what the hell was going on, but I was sober enough to know that no good comes out of a too-much-chardonnay conversation. So I just let him show me how to cut a tomato better. At this point, I just wanted to eat and go to bed and wake up to a new millennium the next day. *It will be fine*, I told myself. All couples have their moments.

When I woke up the following morning, Richard was already gone. I looked at the clock next to the bed: 10:00 a.m.! *I must have had more wine than I realized*, I thought as I slithered out of bed and shuffled to the TV room. Richard was sitting in a club chair next to a fire, rolling calls.

"I just wanted to wish you the best of everything in the New Year. And tell you how much I hope all your wishes come true," he said into the phone. I felt the whole room spin as he turned around in his chair.

"Well, look who is up," he said flatly.

"What are you doing?" I asked.

"Just making all my New Year's calls," he said, before turning back around and dialing someone else, saying the exact same thing he had said to me before we started dating.

A couple of nights after we returned from Vail, I awoke gasping for air. My hands were clutched in bear-claw fists. My feet were prickly and cold. My mouth was devoid of saliva. And my heartbeat was so rapid it caused my throat to tighten and my breath to grow shallow. Panic overtook me. I was afraid I might start screaming and never be able to stop. I thought about waking up Richard. But when I looked over to see if any of my discomfort had disrupted his REM sleep, I found him lying peacefully on his back, his hands across his chest, an almost imperceptible snore coming out of his nose, and decided not to. This was probably for the best, because, as I took him in, I knew (in that way a woman does) that the physical and emotional discomfort that had just hijacked my body was the result of ignoring all the little clues for far too long:

He's not your guy, Amy.

Hopping out of our Japanese-style bed, I opened the sliding glass doors leading out to the balcony to get some air and take in the view. But at 3:00 a.m., all I could see were the twinkling lights of Los Angeles and the strategically lit palm trees that adorned Richard's trophy house. I realized that I was a trophy, too, the person Richard had hoped would complete the picture-perfect life he was trying to build, not the person who was struggling.

As I took in the night sky, my knees began to buckle. I had become so muddled and intertwined with Richard's life and this house that I didn't even have an identity anymore. If I chose to leave, who would I be? Where would I live? I wasn't exactly making any money at the moment. I felt alone and lost and stuck and ashamed.

He's not your guy, Amy.

I walked back inside to wake Richard. But just as I returned to the bed, fearful that I was on the brink of losing every ounce of composure, I knew I had to get back into that pose I had done in class a few months earlier.

I knelt on my hands and knees next to the bed and placed my hands flat on the ground, shoulder-width apart. Then, spreading my fingers wide, I pushed my buttocks up into the air. *You really are a mess*, I thought, as my whole body began to shake, like a car recalibrating, until finally it stopped and, miraculously, my breath grew long and deep, and my racing thoughts subsided. As my heels continued to sink into the ground, I felt as still as the night air. It was the first time I'd felt at home in a long while. I was back in my body, connecting to my first chakra, grounded, just as Sharika had promised.

The following morning, I was in the bathroom applying cover up to the dark, puffy circles under my eyes when Richard walked in. He looked ready to claim gold at the Olympics.

"God, I slept like a rock last night," he said, stretching his arms above his head. I debated whether or not I should tell him about my night as he turned on the shower. But then he turned back around. "You know, I think I'm ready to start construction on the house so you can put it back on the market by this summer. I really want you to sell it for me."

Richard needed me for something again. It wouldn't look right to bail the minute the jackhammer was about to strike.

Plus…I still loved him. At least, a part of me did. And the fact that Richard had just asked me to help him sell his house suggested he still loved and believed in me a little, too.

So, that spring we began demolition on all the windows and doors and balconies on the second floor—what Richard called "phase two" of his construction plan. "There are just no shortcuts," he said, after we'd tested the market to no avail.

Not unless you're Piper Perabo, I thought.

One morning, two months into construction, after a night of howling wind and rain had kept me, not only up all night, but fearful that an intruder might sneak in, I couldn't take it anymore. The only thing covering the whole backside of the second floor was a sheet of plastic, and we were using the gym as a makeshift bedroom, which I locked myself in every night until Richard got home. I stomped into the bathroom. Richard was brushing his teeth.

"When will the walls be back in?" I demanded.

He spit in the sink, careful not to get toothpaste on the side of the basin and looked me straight in the eye through the mirror. "Be a winner, not a whiner," he said, all Buddha-like.

I knew in theory he was right. Construction was a rich man's problem. In the past, whenever I heard about a couple getting a divorce over demolition, I'd thought *shame on them*. But now that I was "the couple" living through demolition, I understood. It's so uprooting, the complete opposite of being grounded in your first chakra. With five guys banging, yelling, and stomping around the clock, it was impossible for me to stay focused on things like maybe still wanting to pursue acting or getting back into downward dog.

Luckily, real estate was keeping me out of the house some of the time. Spring is the busiest time of year for buying and selling homes, and I had two new buyers. One of them was my good friend, Lila, who'd just gone into escrow on an amazing, chic condo off Sunset. The other was a talent agent Richard had referred to me whom I'd already shown a hundred houses to and was still no closer to making a decision. I couldn't help but recognize how, just a few months ago, I was challenged with getting acting roles and reaching my dreams. Now, my biggest challenge was how I should pronounce Realtor. Was it: Reel a tor? Real tour? Or, Reel ah toor?

Then, one morning in early May, I woke to thirteen voicemails from my mom and gained some new perspective on real challenges. I had spent the night at Lila's house after she'd closed on the new condo I sold her. All the girls had gone out the night before to celebrate, and I had been too drunk to drive home.

"Oh, my God," I said, jumping out of Lila's bed, ripping off my PJs and pulling up my jeans with one hand as I listened to one of the voicemails. "My mom's in Orange County right now. My aunt and uncle were in a car accident last night."

"What?" Lila replied, sitting up in bed.

"I gotta go."

"Do you want me to drive you down there?"

"No, Richard will," I said, stuffing the rest of my things into my purse and bolting out the door.

On the way back to Richard's, I called my mom, who informed me in a low, distraught whisper that my uncle Gary was in brain surgery and that her sister, my aunt, who was more like an older sister to me, was also in surgery. Both of them had broken nearly every bone in their bodies and were barely hanging on. Thankfully, my aunt had no head trauma.

"What about Ian?" I screamed through the line. Ian was their six-year-old son. He was the youngest and only boy on my mom's side of the family. The pride and joy in all of our lives.

"He wasn't in the car," my mom said, barely audible.

When I got home, I found Richard reading a script in our bedroom and told him what had happened. I was hysterical, and he was steady and calm, offering all the practical words a surgeon does when he comes out to talk to the family in the waiting room. Then, all I remember is: I started cleaning. I mopped the floors. Unloaded the dishwasher. Did a load of laundry. Until, finally, it hit me: *What am I doing?* And I got in my car and drove to the hospital. Alone.

Over the next month, my life revolved around my aunt and cousin. She was now home and needed around-the-clock care and help with Ian. Nurses came and went daily, but Ian was just a little boy who needed to be loved and nurtured by familiar faces at such a fragile time. My aunt needed that, too. Various family members from out of state were taking turns coming out to help her, but I was the only family member who lived in California, so on the days that rotating visits didn't overlap, it fell on me to be there. My aunt was slowly mending, but my uncle was still in a coma, unresponsive, waiting for his fourth brain surgery.

One night, about five weeks after the accident, Richard walked into the kitchen. I was standing at the counter, sorting through some medical documents for my aunt, exhausted.

"I was thinking of throwing a party here for my birthday next weekend," he said, opening the fridge.

"I'm not much up for a party," I snapped.

"I know," he replied gently. "But maybe you should take your mind off everything for a minute."

It was true. I had been consumed by the family tragedy all month. Maybe Richard needed a little joy in the house. I couldn't fault him for that. He didn't even know my aunt and uncle that well. And, in fairness to him, just last week he'd suggested we have my cousin over some weekend to swim and go to Universal Studios. He said he would get us a VIP pass so we didn't have to wait in any lines.

"Okay, let's have the party," I told him that night. I knew Richard was trying to be there for me. But there was something wrong that I just couldn't pinpoint.

Then, the morning after the party dawned. I was frantically searching my bathroom drawers when Richard walked in, groggy.

"My diamond necklace is gone," I said.

"What do you mean 'gone'?" he asked.

"It was here yesterday. I think someone from the party stole it."

I knew Richard did not like where I was going with this. Over the past few weeks, I'd voiced to him how intimate gatherings with friends and acquaintances were fine with me but that five hundred strangers on our tennis court was becoming too much. I was craving a home full of cozy conversation, not a discothèque. When I finished, I sensed his brain saying, "Who is she—the girl who lived in a small apartment before meeting me—to come in and screw that up?" Richard designed his house for BIG, with its indestructible concrete floors and steel walls.

"Well," he shrugged, "that's what happens when you tempt human nature."

"So this is my fault?"

"You should have put it away before everyone came over."

On a practical level, I knew Richard was right. I should have put my necklace away (although I sort of thought I had when I put it in my drawer). But, "that's what happens when you tempt human nature." Who says that? I didn't want logical advice, I wanted my necklace back, and, at the very least, some small acknowledgment that maybe, just maybe, when you're inviting large masses of people into your home who are stealing from you, it's time to reevaluate how you entertain.

Richard didn't take out insurance on the necklace, so I thought about calling the police. Then I realized "To do what?" I didn't know the names of half the people who came to our parties, and I wasn't about to drag the people I *did* know into some Nancy Drew drama on *The Stolen Necklace*. I wanted a hug.

As I watched Richard brush his teeth in perfect strokes, I had an epiphany. His highly overdeveloped left brain overshadowed the warm, fuzzy instincts most people I was close to had. It's not that Richard was a bad guy. It's just… if I was Pippy Longstocking, Richard was Dr. Spock. Of course, he didn't have pointy ears or jet-black hair but, like Spock, Richard was very precise and logical, in control and unemotional all the time, no matter what. Nothing could ruffle Richard's feathers—not my tears, my dramas, my disappointments, or (what he perceived as) my flaws, even if he didn't admit that he perceived them as flaws because unemotional people always pretend to be non-judgmental. *Here, let me show you how to cut that tomato.*

He might have been a: Designer. Lawyer. Agent. Landlord. But he was not a: Hugger.

A few days after Richard's birthday party, I was in the office surfing the computer for listings when Lila called and asked me if I knew the exact time I was born. She said she had a special gift she wanted to get to me right away. I told her I would find out. Two weeks later, I received a package with a cassette tape inside from an astrologer named David Pond. As soon as I saw David's name, I remembered Lila mentioning how her sister enlisted this guy whenever she needed some direction in her life. I immediately picked up the phone and called her.

"What an interesting gift," I said.

"Well, I've sensed that you've been searching for some (long pause) answers lately," she said delicately.

Even though I usually told my best friends everything, I still hadn't told them about how confused I'd been feeling over Richard. I felt too ashamed to admit any unhappiness when I knew I had a lot to be happy about. And they weren't the type of women to come out and insert their opinion about someone's relationship. That's what they had me for. I was the one in our group who had no filter. But as I studied the tape sitting on the table, obviously I knew that she knew something was up and promised her I'd listen to the tape right away.

"Make sure it's in private," she said before hanging up.

Later that afternoon, I headed up Fryman Canyon for a hike. Full of anticipation, I inserted David's tape into my Walkman and pressed play. He immediately informed me that my chart had a real seesaw grouping of planets: I probably wasn't married (rewind), hadn't found my soul mate yet (rewind), and wasn't going to anytime soon (rewind). He said I probably didn't live in the same town I grew up in, but that I'd been blessed with amazing friendships with all types of women. In a cautionary tone, he said that relationships with men would probably continue to be difficult, but the greatest learning would come from them. Then he informed me that studying the chakras (REWIND—what's the deal with these chakras?) and integrating a spiritual practice would be very good for me. Although he guessed I would not consciously embark on this spiritual journey for at least another decade, he told me that I'd eventually seek it in order to fulfill my soul's journey. He said it would be "the necessary curriculum for my soul to advance in its learning of life's experiences, especially in the area of dating."

As I reached the summit that day, I felt both an overwhelming sense of relief and doom. On the one hand, I was relieved that there was a very good explanation as to why I was the way I was: my planets were fucked up at birth! On the other hand, I felt doomed by the work ahead of me. It sucked being told there was no easy fix and that a soul mate wasn't in my near future. I'm an Aries. Aries want everything to happen fast. "Ready, fire, aim," was how David put it. So that afternoon, as soon as I got home, I threw the tape in a drawer and forgot about it. David had to be wrong.

I put the house back on the market on August 1. That same day, a twenty-five-year-old bigwig from one of the major studios came to look at it with his mom, who was also his Realtor. He told me he wanted to make an offer and asked if he could come back later that night with his whole family to discuss it. Richard came home from work early. There was no way he wasn't going to control the negotiations. After an hour of touring the house, we all ended up in the kitchen like old friends. His dad was really laying it on thick: "Oh, come on, just sign it! You know you want to!"

Richard was flustered—a side of him I hadn't seen before. I told them we needed to discuss their offer in private. There was a vulnerability Richard had allowed to peek through. I felt protective of him. His house was his baby, a labor of love. And I knew it was my turn to step up to the plate.

I turned to him with confidence and said, "Why don't we go down to the tennis court."

"Okay," he replied sheepishly.

For the first time, I was steering the ship in our relationship. As we circled the court, I assured Richard the offer was a good one, almost full price. Still, Richard was hemming and hawing. He told me the only way he would sign the contract was if the buyer agreed to close in thirty days instead of forty-five.

"But we'll be in Italy, on the isle of Capri, in thirty days," I said gently.

He looked stunned. "Oh yeah," he said. "I forgot." And with that, he immediately snapped back to his old self and marched back into the kitchen. He picked up the pen and signed each of the contract's ten pages. "Congratulations," he said to the buyer. "You just got yourself a great house."

The house sold for over three million, the most anyone had ever paid in the neighborhood to date. People started wondering who this new Realtor was who broke the price record in the Hollywood Hills. I felt like I was getting a little bit of my mojo back.

Right after we got the offer, Richard's good friend Ricky asked if he could host his fortieth birthday party at our house. Ricky was in the oil business and very successful. He went to Harvard Business School and looked like Tom Selleck. He always had a devious smirk on his face and was married to a Playboy Playmate. Richard told him yes. It would be his last hurrah at the house.

Ricky's guest list had about fifty people on it. The day of the party, I was helping Richard clean and organize the patio furniture when Sloan called.

"Sweetie," she said. "I just did my romantic resume and it got me thinking…if I want to find a husband, I should be dating men ten years older than me. Anyway, I just wanted to put it out there in case Richard has any friends or events with older friends. Just think of me, please. "

Even though I wasn't in charge of the guest list, her timing was too good not to include her. Plus, it was my house, so I felt it was my right to invite at least one of my friends. I hardly knew anyone on the guest list. I told her to be at our place at 8:00. "Perrrrfect," she said.

Later that night, Sloan and I were dangling our feet in the Jacuzzi, taking in all the people mingling by the pool. I spotted a pair of Gucci loafers (we were eye level to everyone's feet) and followed my gaze up to a handsome guy with salt-and-pepper hair. He was wearing a pair of Oliver People glasses and had a black cashmere sweater tied around his neck. He was talking to a group of three or four people huddled in a circle. I immediately got up and grabbed Sloan by the hand. "Follow me," I said.

Dragging Sloan across the pool deck, I introduced myself as the lady of the house to Mr. Gucci. He said his name was Trent. I asked him how he knew Ricky. He told me they met at Harvard. *Perfect*, I thought pulling Sloan up from behind me. In that moment, I swear I saw Trent get stars in his eyes, and I suggested he join us by the Jacuzzi.

After a little small talk, I realized he and Sloan hardly even knew I was there and excused myself. For the rest of the night, Trent didn't leave her side. I thought it was really telling how fast something can happen when you put yourself out there, like Sloan had when she called me earlier that day to claim exactly what she wanted: a man a decade older.

Practically everyone working in entertainment goes on vacation in August, and Hollywood feels like a ghost town. Things between Richard and me still felt distant. Selling the house represented the end of a big chapter. I was hoping, as I think Richard was, that this trip to Capri would mark the beginning of a new and improved chapter. It was going to be the place where we would fall in love all over again.

When we arrived by ferry to the island of Capri, I was immediately struck by all the colorful homes sprinkled in hillside cliffs overlooking the Gulf of Naples. The water was spectacularly blue but—to my dismay—everywhere I looked, sunbathers were sprawled out on pavement. Where was the sand? The beaches looked like parking lots.

Richard had arranged for us to stay at the private home of one of his biggest clients, a commercial director who had a two-century-old villa on one of Capri's most exclusive streets. It was perched behind a private wood door with patinated cement walls covered in moss. It was, hands down, the most romantic, sophisticated, and enthralling place I had ever seen. And as I took in the mature trees dripping with fruit sprinkled throughout the property, the only thought running through my head was: *I wish I were here with another man, one whom I wanted to caress my naked body by the side of the pool and hand feed me figs because I am so ravenous.*

At this time, Richard and I were not having a lot of sex. In fact, we weren't having any. I didn't know it was possible to feel like a shell of a woman at thirty, but that's how I felt, hollow on the inside and delicate on the outside. I reminded myself of a character I once portrayed in acting class from a book called *Spoon River Anthology*. Spoon River is a fictional town and everyone in it is dead. The book's comprised of characters giving one-page soliloquies about the grievances they feel from the grave. Performing a monologue from this book is pretty standard for anyone taking an acting class based on the teachings of Sanford Meisner. I just think it's interesting that the character I identified with most was one who claimed to feel like a shell of a woman, and I was counting on Capri to change this. In Capri, the very landscape encouraged great sex.

Yet, that first night, Richard was distant and cold, falling asleep next to me just like he did back home: his back to me. As I stared at the ceiling wide-eyed, wearing a pair of boxers and a t-shirt, I wondered if Richard was dreaming about the person he'd rather be lying next to, like I was. So, in a way, it was a relief he didn't try to touch me. But another part of me felt deeply hurt. The part that just wanted to be loved and longed for him to rip off my clothes and throw me onto the floor. I fell asleep determined to go into town to buy a new pair of black lace panties to change all of this.

The following morning, I rolled over and reached for Richard on the opposite side of the bed but was met with his crumpled-up blanket and goose-down pillow. There had been no morning kiss or warm cuddles before he got out of bed and left me. *We are not off to a good start*, I thought, as I slid out of bed and tiptoed across the cold tile floors, over to the window, and peeked out. Richard was lying out by the pool, reading a book in his blue swimming trunks. He looked toned and had tennis player legs. The thing I liked best about Richard's body, though, was his masculine chest. He had the perfect dip and amount of hair on his breastbone.

I pulled a blue sundress out of my suitcase and slithered into it feet first. Unlike Richard, who had already hung up all his clothes in the closet to the left of the bed, I still hadn't unpacked. I would make an effort to be neater, I promised myself, before making my way down to the pool.

"*Buon giorno*," I said, sitting at the foot of Richard's chaise lounge.

"Morning," he replied, not in a mean tone, but more of an indifferent one.

I noticed the little beads of sweat gathering on his chest and thought about straddling him in the chair. But he was acting so distant, I was afraid he'd reject me. I couldn't bear to hear, "Amy, I'm just not attracted to you anymore." We were on an island in the middle of the Mediterranean Sea. There were no trains, planes, or automobiles leaving on the hour that I could hop on, only a little ferry that took me to Naples. From there, I'd have to get to Rome to catch a flight back to L.A., and then what? No. I could not risk getting rejected right then. So, I just told him I was going into town for a cappuccino and asked him if he wanted to come. Of course, he told me he was fine by the pool. Richard was always fine.

I found a sidewalk café next to one of the big hotels and ordered three chocolate croissants with my coffee. An exotic woman with silky black hair pulled back into a low ponytail was popping into Prada across the street. She looked fashionable in her mini skirt and strappy sandals that wrapped all the way up her tanned calves. I wished I could just be the girl whose only goal that day was to buy a Prada backpack (all the rage in 1999-2000) and sunbathe on the cement.

On our last day in Capri, Richard and I decided to explore the island with his camera before the sun went down. I still hadn't made it to that lingerie shop for a pair of panties, and Richard still hadn't tried to throw me on the floor. Making our way down a long, narrow street that dead-ended at the sea, we noticed a single lamppost perched outside one of the hotels overlooking the ocean, along the cliffs. I leaned up against it and inhaled deeply as I stared out at the water. Richard brought the camera up to his eye. He turned to the left and then the right, exploring the perfect shot, before settling it on me. I adjusted my body into a pose against the post and offered him a big smile.

"Would you mind standing over there?" Richard asked nonchalantly, pointing to the right of the post.

"Sure," I replied, only to realize moments later, as I watched him snap several shots of the lightpost with the sea and cliffs in the backdrop, that he didn't want me in the picture. I thought I was going to cry and turned my face in the other direction so Richard wouldn't see me as he continued clicking.

When we got back to Los Angeles, the chaos of moving overwhelmed everything. Richard and I had one week to pack up fifteen rooms, a storage shed, and an acre overflowing with patio furniture. There was no time for break-ups. Come moving day, as I scanned the empty living room for that one last vase we might have forgotten tucked away in the cupboard, suddenly I missed all the parties that drove me nuts, the pool I never swam in, and the tennis court Richard and I never practiced on together once I'd moved in with him. As much as I had thought I was ready to go, now I wasn't sure. I decided to move into the new rental house above the famed Chateau Marmont Hotel with Richard as planned.

One night, about two weeks after moving in, I was sitting on the couch sipping a glass of wine and reading in front of the fire when Richard walked in. The lights were slightly dimmed, giving the room an ambiance that would lead any happy couple to nakedness. Richard sat down next to me and looked my way as if he were about to touch me.

"I think we should get a kitten," he said.

Although I would have preferred a kiss or a golden retriever, his suggestion to get a cat enticed me. Perhaps it would give us something to bond over together. I was desperate to give us one last shot and told him I thought it was a great idea. Two days later, Richard walked into our kitchen with our new Himalayan, Macy Gray. She was cute as could be with her gray and white fur, bright blue eyes, and flattened face. I scooped Macy Gray out of Richard's arms and showered her with pets and kisses. As I poured my love onto her, though, I realized that, like Richard, she was aloof and didn't reciprocate my affection. She and Richard, on the other hand, totally bonded, like they were lovers from a past life. From the very beginning, they were all over each other, and when they weren't, they seemed like identical twins: noses up in the air, heads going from left to right as they scoped out the room, deciding who was worthy of their attention.

A couple nights later, I found Macy Gray and Richard snuggled up together in the very leather club chair in front of the fireplace where I had hoped Richard was going to touch me. He was reading a script and she was purring on his lap. I hadn't fully realized how capable Richard still was of giving affection or that Macy Gray was interested in receiving it until I watched the two of them together that night in our living room: kisses on the nose, baby talk into the ears, and massages on the stomach, followed by contented purrs. When I sat down in the club chair next to them, I finally understood what every man in

America must feel as he watches his wife breastfeed: I was out. Richard liked Macy Gray better.

The following night, Richard took me to dinner at Ruth's Chris Steak House in Beverly Hills. After the waiter poured our cabernet, and we raised our glasses for a toast, I blurted, "I think we should break up." I was surprised by how easily the words flew out of my mouth. Richard wasn't surprised in the least, though.

"I think it's for the best," he replied, taking my hand underneath the table.

We looked into each other's eyes and smiled. It was as if (and I hate to throw out a cliché) the truth had set us free to love each other in a real way. And, in that moment, I wondered why we hadn't been honest earlier. Perhaps if we had, we wouldn't be breaking up now.

That night, we didn't make love one last time or have breakup sex, but we did cuddle like two people trying to save each other from getting frostbite. The whole night, Richard held onto me so tight, I began to question if he really wanted to break up. Then the cuddling abruptly ended in the morning and Richard jumped out of bed. It was a Saturday and he was off to play basketball. The guy who bought his house had continued hosting the game on the tennis court. "I assume you can manage getting out your stuff," he said flatly as he leaned down to give me a final peck before leaving.

I thought it was cold-hearted that he hadn't offered to help me move some things out. As I looked around, I realized that, other than my clothes, the only thing I owned in this whole house was a jute rug.

CHAKRA TWO

Matt
May 2001- February 2002

"The experiences of the second chakra
provide the first taste of merger, of going
beyond one's isolated self, dissolving
with, through, and into another."
—The Aquarian Teacher

As fate would have it, my standup comedian friend Annie had a spare bedroom she needed to rent out in West Hollywood. Annie and I were roommates our sophomore year in college. We'd lost touch a little after we graduated. She moved to San Francisco; I moved back to Chicago. Then, within one month of each other, we both moved to L.A., independently, to pursue acting. She was like family to me. So the timing of my breakup with Richard and our good friend Polly moving out because she'd just sold her first screenplay couldn't have been better. We often referred to each other as Frick and Frack.

When I walked up to Annie's doorstep that day, my jute rug in tow, I was struck by how much my soon-to-be-home reminded me of the one we shared back in college, six years earlier. There were dead plants in the flower boxes, rusty aluminum awnings above the windows, and a pile of paint chips on the ground. Still, the moment I rang the bell and Annie answered, I didn't feel like I was going backwards.

"Frick!" she proclaimed with outstretched arms.

"Frack," I replied dropping my rug to the ground and stepping inside, where suddenly it all became so real: the tired floors, the non-working fireplace, and the old stucco walls. I was officially living the life of a commoner again.

When we were college roommates, Annie and I played interior decorator every other week. We would test a new paint color on the wall, move the plant to various corners of the room, or recover some old throw pillow. Finding a spot for my jute rug meant immediately falling into that old routine.

Without even speaking, I moved a chair toward the window as Annie pushed the coffee table to the far corner of the room. I heard a loud scratching sound echo off the walls because Annie had failed to put something underneath the coffee table's legs to protect the floors. Bringing me to one of the major reasons why our constant redecorating/rearranging drove our other college roommate crazy: Nine times out of ten, Annie and I were so excited to see the new and improved look that we rushed or abandoned the job at hand. Just like how I was always "almost" famous" in Hollywood; our apartments together were always "almost" decorated.

I walked over and helped Annie lift the table into the dining room. Then we kneeled on opposite sides of my jute rug and unrolled it in front of Annie's flower-patterned sofa and stood back, silently taking in the room together. It was a far cry from the lavish, multi-million-dollar Hollywood Hills home I'd grown accustomed to living in with Richard. Yet, the moment I entered my new bedroom that afternoon, I fanned my arms out like I was about to make a snow angel and fell back onto the bed with a smile on my face. I was exactly where I should be. I felt free, supported, and alive for the first time in a long while.

A month after moving in with Annie, Polly invited me out to celebrate the sale of her screenplay with her new manager, Russ. I was the one who'd passed her script on to Russ while I was dating Richard. Richard did a lot of business with Russ's Oscar successful wife Eden. One night, the four of us went out to dinner together. During the course of the conversation, it came up that Russ had just started a new management company for writers. Coincidentally, I had just finished reading Polly's script that week, so I suggested she send it over to him. She did, and within two weeks Russ took her on as a client and got her script sold for well into the six figures (the reason the other room at Annie's opened up).

We decided to celebrate the sale at the latest Hollywood nightclub on Vine. The place was packed with Hollywood hipsters and the house music vibrated my chest, as smoke loomed all around us on the dance floor. I told Polly I had to get some air, but she was bumping hips with some hot guy, oblivious to the cloud of nicotine overhead. Shimmying my way past dozens of moving arms and legs, trying not to get hit, I finally reached a thick red velvet rope that separated the dance floor from the bar area and came up to my waist.

"Need some help with that?" a random guy's voice wafted over.

Reaching for his already extended hand, I felt a current of electricity the moment our palms met and looked up. A hunk with twinkling, pale blue eyes and broad shoulders was staring back at me. He looked like he belonged at a writers' conference in Vermont with his gray t-shirt, cut-off khakis and Birkenstocks-not a Hollywood bone in his body. Still holding his hand, I hopped over the rope.

"Amy, this is my friend Matt," Russ said, approaching from behind with two drinks in his hand.

"That was an impressive hop," Matt smiled, revealing the cutest dimples I'd ever seen in my life.

"I was a hurdle jumper in high school," I said.

"Really?"

"Actually, no. I was on the tennis team," I said, catching myself. *I hope he doesn't own a tennis court.*

Russ told me Matt had just moved to L.A. from New York. I asked how he liked it so far.

"There are really good oranges here," he said.

Who was this adorable guy without a jaded Hollywood bone in his body? I wanted to find out more about him and suggested we head out to the patio and get some fresh air. Russ told us to find a table while he went to fetch Polly, who was still on the dance floor, moving like a break-dancer on crack.

The corridor leading out to the courtyard patio was narrow and dark. Matt turned around and offered his hand to me for a second time. Once again, the moment our palms touched, my skin responded in that way one can only hope for when there's chemistry. Now that I felt more grounded in my home life, perhaps other parts of me were coming back to life as well.

After finding a table in front of an outdoor fireplace with little votive candles running all along the mantle, Matt told me he was an aspiring screenwriter and had just moved to L.A. a couple of months before. He said he was looking for an agent but hadn't published or sold anything yet. I knew from my pursuit of acting that the road ahead of him wasn't going to be easy. Unlike Richard, who had ten thousand people in his Rolodex, Matt told me he didn't really know anyone in L.A., but I wasn't about to burst his bubble. Perhaps he had some family connections that would hook him up in the television world. But after telling me he grew up in Ohio, I wasn't sure how that was possible.

Still, it was refreshing. I liked being able to talk freely with someone about the business versus being schooled by someone about the business. Just because we hadn't "made" it yet didn't mean we didn't know a lot about our respective crafts or that we weren't talented. Crossing my arms in front of my chest, I gave my upper arms a quick rub as a breeze took out the candles. Matt got up and draped the sweater that had been tied around his waist over my shoulders.

"How's that?" he asked, his blue eyes twinkling.

"Perfect," I said.

The following morning, Polly called to ask if it was okay if Russ passed my number on to Matt. So it wasn't a total surprise when a New York area code popped up on my cell screen later in the day.

"How's my favorite hurdle jumper?"

A sheet of goose pimples covered my arms as I listened to Matt's deep, husky voice. He asked if I was going to Russ's barbeque on Saturday. When I told him I was, he offered to pick me up. Even though I was very excited over this man who had seemingly fallen into my universe out of nowhere, I always liked to have my own "getaway" car on a first date—just in case. I told him I'd meet him there.

That Saturday, I meandered my way through Russ's kitchen on the way to the backyard, discreetly looking for Matt amongst the seventy people there. I didn't see him but bumped into Eden. She was chatting with a group of gals she appeared to have wrapped around her finger. I said hello, and it was all she could do to smile at me. In fact, she seemed utterly annoyed that I was there. Then Matt walked up and her whole demeanor changed. She gave him a hug and introduced him to her friends, explaining how they all went to prep school together—all without ever looking at me. I felt like pond scum until Matt made his way over to me, flashing that infectious, glistening smile.

"Hi, Amy," he said, giving my shoulder an affectionate squeeze. "Should we go grab a drink?"

On the way to the bar, I asked him how he knew Eden. He told me they had a lot of friends in common, sharing that he probably had more in common with her than Russ. "We have similar backgrounds," he offered, before asking me what I wanted to drink. I told him a chardonnay, but the line was now forty-people deep.

"Want to get out of here? Go up to my place?" he asked.

"Nothing sounds better," I blurted rather quickly for a girl who insisted on having her own getaway car.

We decided I would follow Matt to his house. When we reached my blue Volvo, Matt seemed instantly giddy, telling me to wait there, that he was just across the street another few cars up and would pull around. When he drove up next to my car a few moments later, huge smiles spread across our faces simultaneously. We both drove Volvos. It was pretty cute. No guys in L.A. drove Volvos, especially not the maroon station wagon model Matt had. I put on my glasses and gave Matt the thumbs up that I was ready. *Ready to jump his bones.*

Matt lived in Beachwood Canyon, which had a bohemian vibe and was located under the Hollywood sign. His house was nestled in the hillside, surrounded by trees. It looked like a cabin that belonged in the Northeast. The inside reflected the same energy. Between the wood bookcases, beamed ceilings, Persian rugs, and piles of *New York Times* stacked in the corner, it was everything Richard's home was not: cozy, traditional, and… (I was happy to observe) a little messy. It felt like a place where a journalist for *National Geographic* would live. I knew from selling real estate that the rent on this place wasn't cheap. Russ mentioned that Matt was from an affluent town in Ohio. Perhaps he did have some family connections in Hollywood.

Hanging on the wall were several pictures of Matt with two studious-looking, dark-haired women in wire-framed glasses and thick cable-knit sweaters. The antithesis of L.A. girls, neither wore a speck of make-up. "Those are my sisters," he said, walking up with two glasses of wine. I'd never been so relieved to be wearing my glasses on a first date. I'd heard men date girls who are the opposite of their sisters but tend to marry girls who are like them. I told Matt they looked really smart. He told me one was in graduate school at Harvard, and the other had gone to Wellesley.

As we continued down the wall of framed pictures, I couldn't help but wonder if I might be too L.A. for him. Then he put his mouth on mine, and any thought of his sisters melted away. As he leaned me back onto his couch, I nonchalantly pulled off my glasses and placed them on the floor next to me. It was getting pretty heated as he flipped us onto the floor and...CRUNCH! Matt pulled my glasses out from underneath him and held them up. They looked like a pretzel. I was kind of bummed as Matt resumed kissing me. The moment was a little ruined. I had waited two weeks for those glasses to come in and didn't know how I'd be able to drive home without them. I thought now might be a good time to slow it down and sat up. I knew it was a total accident, but I still wasn't going to sleep with him on a first date, which wasn't technically even a first date since we had both been invited to Russ and Eden's barbeque. I told him I had to get going and thanked him for a great evening.

First thing the following morning, my phone rang. "Sorry about your glasses," Matt said with sincerity. I told him it wasn't his fault, but he insisted on making it up to me by cooking me dinner. The following night, I threw on a pair of black skinny jeans and heels and headed back to Matt's house. When I entered his kitchen, Matt was listening to public radio and arranging smoked salmon on a platter. His hands looked strong and masculine. I set the bottle of wine I'd brought on the counter. Before I could say hello, he placed a piece of salmon on a toast point in my mouth. His finger tasted salty. I wanted to melt. He was so sexy. He turned back toward the sink to grab a wine glass. There was a window that looked out toward his wooded backyard. He abruptly put down the glass and grabbed a flashlight from his kitchen drawer instead. "A deer!" he shouted.

I looked out the window and saw a set of yellow eyes staring back at me. Matt took my hand and steered us outside. It seemed the deer was long gone but this didn't stop Matt. "Follow me," he said, turning on the flashlight and heading up the yard.

The minute my feet hit the hillside, my heels sunk into the mud and I wished I'd worn my running shoes. *First my glasses, now my Jimmy Choos,* I thought, as Matt turned off his flashlight and gasped. Looking up from the ground, I saw a whole family of deer staring back at me, their eyes glowing in the dark.

It was pretty "out there" as far as second dates go. But after so many premieres and swanky Hollywood dinners, trekking deer felt kind of refreshing, too. I could feel that Colorado girl inside me coming back to life.

I made my way over to one of Matt's bookcases in the living room and perused his collection of hardcovers.

"Do you like Raymond Carver?" Matt asked, walking up from behind with a glass of wine. I felt the heat of his breath on my neck and admitted I hadn't read much by him. Matt pulled a compilation of Carver's short stories off the top shelf and walked over to the couch. Patting the little throw pillow he had just placed in his lap after taking a seat on the far right corner of the sofa, he told me to come lie down. I rested my head in his lap, and Matt opened the book above me and began to read aloud.

I closed my eyes and listened to the words roll off Matt's tongue. There wasn't a hint of self-consciousness in his voice as he read each sentence in perfect iambic pentameter with the ease of a Shakespearian actor. No man had ever read to me before. I was amazed how this simple gesture electrified me. He placed his hand on the nape of my neck and leaned down and put his mouth on mine. It felt so reassuring. I didn't want it to end.

My hand in his, I followed Matt up a narrow wooden staircase. The breeze off the balcony felt cool against my face as he gently leaned me down on his bed with one hand and took off my shirt with the other. He paid close attention to my neck and earlobe with his mouth, before bringing his body into mine and looking into my eyes.

And…

I finally understood what all those ladies at the luncheon had been talking about. Never before had I merged into someone else so easily. It was sublime and transcendent and empowering in every way. Until this point, I'd never been the girl who experienced earth-shattering orgasms that started in her toes and exploded out of her eyeballs like some girls I knew. I would often say—after hearing one of my girlfriends brag about her volcanic eruptions of pleasure at a luncheon, probably out of defensiveness or jealousy—"What's the big deal?"

Now, when Matt told me how amazing I was in the sack, I felt like the ugly duckling that had turned into the swan. It was extraordinary to think how one man could make me feel like a dead fish while another could proclaim me to be some sort of Yahweh.

Over the next week, I practically lived at Matt's house. One morning, I rolled over on my stomach and turned my head to the side to meet Matt's gaze. Our eyes locked. It was a perfect moment I wanted to last forever. But Matt abruptly told me it was time to go. He said he liked to be at his computer writing by 9:00 each day. I rolled out of bed and got dressed. Although it was time to reenter the world, being told it was time to leave hurt my feelings a little.

When I approached my front door an hour later, a large envelope from Amazon was leaning against it. I had no idea who it was from and pulled out…*Short Stories* by Raymond Carver. Inside the jacket was a message from Matt that read, "To the prettiest girl in L.A." I brought it close to my chest and smiled.

Crawling into bed that night, I was ecstatic to be in a pair of flannel pajamas and a green facemask. Even though my feelings had been hurt a little that Matt had been the one to initiate the "time to go" episode, I didn't realize how ready I was to be back in my own space. Annie peeked around my bedroom door. I felt a little guilty. After breaking up with Richard, we both talked about how excited we were to be single girls together. And, here I was—just eight weeks after moving in with her—with Matt. A part of me felt very impolite about this, but another part thought, *well…I guess this is what happens when a thirty-two-year-old woman gets in touch with her second chakra for the first time.*

Annie sat down at the base of my bed; we began catching up on our weeks. Then my phone rang. I knew it had to be Matt because no friends called after 10:00 on a Monday. I gestured with my index finger for Annie to hold on for one second, before picking up the phone.

"Can you come over?" Matt pleaded on the other end. He sounded really down.

"Are you okay?"

"I could just use some company."

"I'm really tired, babe."

I looked up at Annie who was gently closing my door behind her.

Matt told me he'd just found out that his dad was sick and that he didn't feel like seeing anyone but me. After spending seven nights together, all of which were bliss, I asked him if I could come over first thing in the morning.

"Please, Amy," he said.

I told him I was on my way.

When I entered the dining room with an overnight bag in tow, Annie was sitting at the table paying bills. I could tell she didn't approve.

"I'm so tired," I said.

"Maybe you need a little space. You've been at his place nonstop."

"I already told him I'd come. See you tomorrow?"

"Uh huh," she replied in a tone that screamed, *I doubt that very much.*

And she was right...

For the rest of the summer, I passed all my days and nights at Matt's house: I lounged on his bed, read books on his couch, took bubble baths in his tub, and drank too many glasses of chardonnay on his patio. I was living off the commission I made selling Richard's house, taking a time-out from acting class, real estate, and friends.

One night in mid-August, we were in Matt's kitchen. He was pulling some smoked salmon out of the fridge to go with a bottle of wine we still hadn't opened.

"You know, why don't we go out tonight, mix things up a little?" I said. "Maybe I could call Annie and Polly to join us. It would be fun."

"I'd prefer to hang out here. We have a lot of good food," he said.

"Okay, then why don't we invite some friends up?"

"I don't know. I'd rather just hang with you."

I realized that, other than Polly's writing manager, Matt still didn't have any friends in L.A., and the next morning I began to wonder if that would ever change. We were in his dining room, which he'd turned into a makeshift office. Stacks of dusty *New York Times* newspapers were stacked on the floor and

National Geographic magazines littered the dining table, which was pushed against the wall. Matt was sitting at his tiny desk, tucked in the opposite corner. I told him it was almost 9:00 and time for me to go. Walking over to his desk, I gave him a peck on the cheek and told him I'd check in with him after my mom arrived in town the next day.

"Why don't you bring her up for lunch tomorrow?" he suggested. Although I thought this was a really nice gesture, I told him we'd play it by ear and that she might be tired from the flight. But, in reality, I just wanted some space.

A couple of days later, Matt ushered us into his living room. He brought my mom and me two grilled cheese sandwiches on pretty plates. As soon as he left the room to go get our drinks, my mom mouthed "He's darling." But I was beginning to feel like I might turn into Ted Kaczynski if I stayed holed up in the woods much longer. I needed to get back to my life, my work, and my acting classes. Yet, no matter how hard I tried, I could never bring myself to leave, sort of like how you can't stop eating all the Thanksgiving leftovers even though you're stuffed.

At the end of August, I was out on Matt's patio when Sloan called. I hadn't seen her for most of the summer.

"Trent proposed!" she exclaimed, before asking me to be one of her bridesmaids.

One morning in early September, Matt shook my leg and told me to wake up. Sitting at the foot of the bed, fumbling for a TV channel, he seemed alarmed. A small plane had hit the World Trade Center, he said. His mom had just called to tell him.

Even in my groggy state, I knew that didn't make sense. Why on earth would a pilot take his plane so far off the grid? *Was he showing off? Did he have a heart attack?* I sat up to join him and together we watched a taped replay of the crash. *Wait. That wasn't such a small plane.* It looked big—more like a commercial aircraft. And it just tore a gaping hole into the North Tower.

Matt gasped, and I shot to the foot of the bed as a ball of black smoke took over the New York skyline. *How could this be happening? Had the steering panel failed?* My uncle, a commercial pilot, once told me that if any mechanical stuff went out on a large aircraft, a pilot could steer the plane manually. All I could do was pray that not too many people were hurt. Still grappling with what we'd just witnessed, a new image interrupted my jumbled thoughts: a second jumbo jet crashed into the South Tower. I jumped up from the bed in horror. This was no accident.

A red-headed news broadcaster I recognized named Carol Marin began recounting the events she'd witnessed on the ground. She had black soot all over her face. Behind her, people ran and screamed. The last I knew, Carol was the local anchor for NBC in Chicago, where my dad had been a reporter for over a decade. Panic overrode everything, even my ability to understand her words. Somewhere in the background, I registered the crescendo of car alarms, but where were they coming from? Was this still New York on the screen? Or did Carol's face on the screen mean a plane had hit Chicago, too?

Running downstairs for my cell phone, I called my mom and dad to make sure they were okay. I reached my mom first. Her voice was shaking. She said she was just about to call me and confirmed that Chicago was still intact and that the family was okay. The Sears Tower was being evacuated. We promised to stay in close touch throughout the day. I told her I loved her and ran back upstairs to be with Matt.

In the bedroom, Matt was cradling his head with both hands. I wrapped my arms around him and listened to the television reports. At 8:46 a.m. Eastern time, American Airlines Flight 11, headed from Boston to Chicago, had hit the North Tower. Not quite twenty minutes later, at 9:03 a.m., United Airlines Flight 175, also headed to Los Angeles from Boston, struck the South Tower. It looked like an extremist group on a suicide mission was responsible, but the details were still unclear. At 9:30 a.m., President Bush came on television from Sarasota and informed the nation that the country had suffered an "apparent terrorist attack." He was very somber and made it sound like the attacks were over.

But by the time Matt and I made our way down to the TV in the living room, newscasters were reporting that a third plane had hit the Pentagon. As that horror sank in, the cameras shifted back to the South Tower collapsing like a child's sandcastle. Then came word that a fourth plane had crashed into a field in Pennsylvania—probably aiming for the White House but somehow diverted.

Watching the North Tower crumble before my eyes, causing a tidal wave of shrapnel to plummet through the streets of New York, I went completely numb. The magnitude of it all was too much for me to process. It didn't seem possible that it could be real. Then I heard a thud come from the TV. Had ten minutes passed or two hours? I wasn't sure. I just remember thinking that a cameraman must have been knocked over and asked Matt what it was.

"Those are bodies," he said, his voice echoing my own despair.

Earlier film coverage from the ground of people falling and jumping from the burning towers had made its way to the airwaves, he told me. No longer numb, I started to scream. *Why didn't anyone do anything to help them? Send up helicopters or parachutes? Set up trampolines on the ground?* Of course, there was nothing anyone could have done. But as I heard another body fall, I covered my ears and ran out of the room sobbing. That was someone's mother, brother, daughter, son, wife, husband, sister, friend, fiancé, grandmother, grandfather, aunt, uncle, and cousin. And it was too much to bear. I felt so helpless and scared and sad.

Throughout the day, as news trickled in, Matt and I tried to comfort each other: a hug, a tender word or touch. But for the most part, we were each struggling separately with our own grief. Matt said he wished he still lived in New York and felt guilty that he wasn't there; I felt guilty that New York was the last place I wanted to be. I imagined myself running away to some small town and never stepping foot in a city again. What should have brought us together somehow opened a gulf between us. After a while, we each retreated to separate rooms.

When I left Matt's the following morning to go home, there was still the typical bumper-to-bumper traffic going down Sunset, but something was different. No one was honking or cutting each other off. Instead, each driver gave way to the other in much the same way that the bus gives way to the rickshaw that gives way to the holy cow in New Delhi. There was camaraderie among my brethren that I had never witnessed before: a friendly wave, a nod of the head, a faint smile. Yet, with these gestures of humanity was a sort of zombie-like quality behind everyone's eyes. It was as if everyone's soul had been crushed, but their hearts had opened up. It was touching and disturbing at the same time. I could hear a pin drop, the streets were so quiet.

The minute I walked through my front door, I embraced Annie. Polly was over, and it looked like the two of them had set up fort on the couch and hadn't moved since yesterday. They both looked exhausted, but Annie seemed particularly drained. She was from the East Coast, waiting to hear if anyone she knew had died in the attacks.

Over the next couple of days—as news coverage of the victims' final moments with loved ones poured in and the reality of what happened sunk in—it got harder, not easier, for me emotionally. Although each story touched my heart so hard I thought it might crumble into a million pieces, there was one man's story in particular that I couldn't get out of my head. He was one of the passengers who had attempted to take on the hijackers and get back control of the plane before it crashed into the field in Pennsylvania. Right before running down the plane's aisle to tackle them, he said, "Let's roll." His wife told the news anchor that it was a catchphrase he always used to psych himself up for a big moment. What a courageous man he was to be able to recall these words in such a moment. How afraid all those passengers must have been.

After a couple of weeks of grappling with my shock and sadness, I needed something to ground me—the solid, constant calm of nature. I asked Matt to come with me on a hike. He declined, saying again that he wished he still lived in New York. It felt like a rebuke and made me feel like a bad person for suggesting it. Matt wasn't ready to move out of any of his pain yet, but I desperately needed to clear some of the darkness festering inside me. I told him I was going to hike Runyon Canyon alone.

"Please don't go," he said.

He looked so sad that I agreed to stay. Like him, like everyone, I still carried the weight of that day. But I also knew that nothing I did could change what happened. And I would lose my mind if I didn't shift my focus. I decided to go to class at Playhouse West.

I hadn't been in over a month and thought maybe I could apply some of the agitation I was feeling to a scene or improvisation. I needed to dump my feelings somewhere. At class that Thursday afternoon, I learned that some of my classmates had written a play about the effect 9/11 had on romantic relationships and were putting it up that weekend. The lead was a beautiful blonde ten years my junior named Danielle. I invited Matt to come with me. To my surprise, he told me he would love to.

The whole play was about two hours long and was really touching. At the end, I went up to say hello to the cast. When I introduced Matt to Danielle, I noticed them make eye contact for a little too long. Matt had this little twinkle in his eyes, and she had this smile on her face that seemed a little too familiar to use with someone you just met. I didn't know if I was being paranoid and didn't say anything to him. With everything that had just happened, it seemed trivial and almost childish to bring it up.

Sloan's wedding was in mid-October. Surprisingly, she was the most low-maintenance bride ever. She didn't have shower after shower, nor did she make the bridesmaids buy dresses. She told us to wear any black one already hanging in our closet that we felt pretty in. Her only request was that we all wear black, closed-toe shoes.

The rehearsal dinner was at a fancy social club downtown. Most of my friends had never met Matt.

I was excited to introduce him to everyone. The first person I saw when Matt and I arrived was Sloan's dad, Willy. The last time I saw Willy was when Richard and I stayed with them in Vail for New Year's two years before. It felt like no time had passed. He looked exactly the same and was as gregarious as I remembered.

"Destiny DNA!" he said in a booming voice. That was the temporary name of a script idea Sloan and I threw around one day in Vail while writing our "B minus" version of Swingers, and he never let us live it down! "How's my little Amy?"

I told him I was great.

"And who's this handsome guy?"

I turned toward Matt. He seemed uncomfortable as he shifted from one foot to another, his jowls tightening. I immediately felt like I needed to put a lid on the joking with Willy. So, after I introduced them, I suggested we go find our name cards.

We were seated at a table with all the other bridesmaids. One of the bridesmaids, who came in from New York, looked just like Allie McGraw. She had long dark hair and porcelain skin. I caught Matt staring at her from across the table. Within minutes, they struck up a conversation about New York. It wasn't an inappropriate connection in light of everything that happened over 9/11, but it was a connection I couldn't share since I'd never lived there. I decided at least he was talking. Up until meeting Allie McGraw, I don't think Matt had said more than twenty words, so I just decided to be grateful that he was loosening up and moved on. I couldn't tell if he was just overwhelmed by everyone's energy or if he just didn't care for the energy of the people that were there.

Halfway into the salad course, the glasses started clinking. It was speech time. The first person to stand up was Sloan's maid of honor, Barbara. She and Sloan used to work together in New York. They were inseparable ever since Barbara had moved to L.A. a few months before. She was the exact opposite of me: very *Sex and the City* with the clothes and the air kisses. Anyway, she gave this really sweet speech about how much Sloan meant to her. When she finished, I was dying to get up and spill my guts about how much Sloan had meant to me over the last several years. Out of anyone, I had the best and most recent stories of her. But I froze and didn't get up to share any of them. I had never had a fear of public speaking before. But I felt like I couldn't be my goofy self in front of Matt. Though I knew it wasn't Matt's fault, his discomfort spilled over to me. I felt stifled somehow, though a part of me realized I was the one stifling myself to avoid overwhelming him. For the rest of the night, I regretted that I didn't say anything.

The following day, all the bridesmaids were invited to get ready at the hotel where Sloan was staying. When I arrived to the suite, Sloan's mom was pouring out bottles of non-alcholic wine in the sink and passing them down to a couple of the bridesmaids who poured regular wine back into the empty bottles using a funnel. The church reception hall "was dry" explained Sloan's mom, in a rather chilly tone—so they were "sneaking in" the real stuff. Although people are always on edge right before a wedding, my gut knew she was disappointed in me for not giving a speech the night before.

The church where Sloan and Trent were getting married was nestled in the cliffs of Palos Verdes, overlooking the ocean. Although I had never been there before, something about it felt ominously familiar. I found out later that the famous scene with the helicopter rising up from the water to rescue James Bond standing on that very cliff was shot there, and it all made sense.

About an hour after arriving and checking out the grounds, Barbara ushered the bridesmaids inside the church to line us up for the procession. When Sloan walked up a few minutes later, my heart was bursting with nostalgia. I immediately told her how beautiful she looked.

"My only request was closed-toe shoes," she snapped, looking down at my feet.

Of course, Barbara was right there to save the day. She reached over to a small table next to Sloan and passed me a shoebox.

"I brought an extra pair," she said with a look of disdain.

For the second time that weekend, I had disappointed Sloan.

Clinging to the idea that at least I was the one who set Sloan up with the man she was about to spend her life with, I proceeded down the aisle. Gripping my toes into the soles of Barbara's shoes with each step I took so I wouldn't fall out of them, I felt like I'd lost my best friend. To add salt to the wound, Matt seemed extra quiet and disconnected from me when we got back to his house. Was it because being at a wedding together reinforced for him that he was nowhere near that chapter in his life? Or did he just not like my friends? Then we tumbled into bed with one another and it felt like we were one again.

Over the next month, anytime I suggested we get out, Matt told me he'd rather just hang at his house. I was beginning to feel like a recluse all holed up in Beachwood Canyon. I couldn't wait to head back to Chicago for Christmas and be surrounded by family and friends. I was ready to be social. Ready to jump out of my skin.

The first week of December, Matt's parents called to tell him that his Christmas present was an all-expense paid trip for two to Hawaii. They said they'd decided to go to London on their own for the holidays. Although grateful for the generous gesture, Matt was sad not to spend Christmas with his parents. No one knew how many Christmases his dad had left. I immediately invited him to go back to Chicago with me, but he shot that idea down pretty quickly, telling me he'd be uncomfortable because he didn't know my family. He asked me to come to Hawaii. After a brief silence, I told him I'd go. "Don't want to twist your arm," he responded sarcastically.

A couple of nights before our trip, I walked into Matt's kitchen and told him to turn around and not peek. When his back was to me, I dragged in two wooden stools from Pottery Barn wrapped in big red bows and tucked them underneath the counter. I really wanted to reciprocate for the all-expense paid trip and had spent a lot of time looking for a pair that had the rustic charm of his house. But when I told him to open his eyes, a stunned look spread across his face, and not a good stunned either.

"You don't like them," I said.

"No. It's just so extravagant," he said.

I was really offended because I knew with every ounce of my being that what he was really saying was that we weren't serious enough for me to have gotten him furniture. Yet here he was, taking me to the tropics. I really resented the double standard and was about to tell him so when he came up and told me he was sorry. "I'm just not used to receiving such extravagant presents. My family gifts each other with things like books." *Was he frickin' serious right now?* It seemed nothing was working but the sex.

Getting to Hana required two separate planes. We had to take a commercial flight to Maui, then hop on a puddle jumper to Hana. The minute I saw the puddle jumper, I was ill at ease. It resembled the one Amelia Earhart disappeared in over the Atlantic. It had rusty wings, old-school propellers, and only seated two. The pilot was dressed in street clothes.

"Can't we take a boat?" I asked.

"It will be fine, Amy."

Several hours after landing in Maui, we arrived in Hana. The multi-acre property's main building was set back on an expansive lawn, surrounded by tropical trees, and the pool was perched on a cliff overlooking the ocean. Golf carts were lined up like grocery carts outside of reception—they were the required modes of transportation to get from Point A to Point B on the property. The hotel's restaurant was probably a twenty-minute walk from our cabana; the pool, a fifteen-minute walk from the reception; and the refreshment stand, a thirty-minute walk from the pool. And, still...we hadn't seen a single soul. When Matt and I entered the lobby, I asked the concierge where everyone was.

"We're in the process of new ownership, so the staff's in transition," she confessed.

Then I saw our room and relaxed. The doors opened out to a balcony right over the ocean. *Now we're talking*, I thought. *This I could get used to.*

After Matt tipped the bellboy, he immediately shut the drapes and crawled into bed. *Nothing like a sexy nap to kick-start our tropical vacation*, I thought. Ready to slip off my sundress, I waited for Matt to invite me to join him. Instead, he turned his back to me and said he wanted to take a nap. It felt like a punch in the gut, but I let it go. Maybe he was legitimately tired from all the traveling. Luckily, I brought Marilyn Monroe's four-hundred-page biography with me. I knew Matt would be armed with an arsenal of literature and wanted to be prepared, just in case. While he slept, I went out on the balcony and read until the sun went down.

Come 9:00 p.m., I was starving and asked Matt if he would get up and go to dinner with me, but he refused to leave the room, complaining of a back-ache. Making the most of what was beginning to feel like a solo trip to Hawaii, I threw on a sundress and began the twenty-minute trek to the lobby restaurant alone. The grounds were pitch black, and I didn't see a soul the whole way there. I felt utterly deserted and alone. The two things I could always count on to share with Matt were good sex and a good meal. Now, even those things were gone. Our relationship was deteriorating before my eyes.

Two days later, Matt suggested we head to the bamboo forest and go hiking. I was ecstatic he wanted to do something and quickly threw on my walking gear. Perhaps once Matt got his blood flow-ing, things would look up. But Matt didn't say a peep to me during the hour-drive there; and, during the hike, he walked way ahead of me. I wanted to parachute off the cliff back to L.A., but, like Capri, I was stranded on this little island with no one to talk to and nowhere to go. It was *deja vu* all over again. Interesting how two totally different guys could pro-duce the same outcome.

As soon as we got back to the hotel room, Matt drew the shades and crawled into bed to take his hun-dredth nap since arriving. I headed to the pool. To my delight, there was another couple lounging on a chaise. I put my stuff on the chair right next to them, but as soon as I rolled out my towel they got up and left hand in hand. They were obviously newlyweds in their own little bubble and wanted absolutely noth-ing to do with me. At least I had Marilyn. Pulling my biography out of my bag, I read very slowly. It was the only book I brought, and I only had one chapter left. I must have read it three times over the next couple of days. I couldn't believe Matt would treat me like this over Christmas when I had changed my plans to come here with him. Clearly, he wasn't into me anymore, and I was utterly confused about what could have happened between inviting me to Hawaii and now. Maybe it was the stools. Whatever it was, I was really hurt and angry, but I didn't have the courage to confront him because all the outbound flights back to California were sold out. I've never felt lonelier than I did on this trip.

When we finally landed back in Los Angeles, Matt didn't say a word from the time we deplaned to the time he turned onto my street. I wanted to punch him, but instead I asked him if he wanted to stay over. I was really asking, "Are we breaking up?" But characters in movies and in all the plays I'd rehearsed never say what they mean, so why should I be any different?

"Actually, this whole thing is moving a little fast for me," he said, as he turned into my driveway and walked me to the door.

"So that's it then?"

"Look, I don't want there to be bad feelings," he said, placing my suitcase on the landing and turning to go.

As I fumbled for my keys at the bottom of my bag and watched him walk away, I knew at least this time around I didn't walk away with just a jute rug. I now owned what all those other girls at the luncheon owned: the tingling sensation in my toes, my hands, and the nape of my neck. I could lunch with the best of them.

Still…

Over the next couple of weeks, I couldn't eat or sleep. And all I did was cry. I would order a pizza and cry. Say hi to the mailman and cry. Watch an episode of *Seinfeld* and cry. Read an email and cry. It seemed my tears were inexhaustible and, after going through my tenth box of Kleenex, I thought it was time to get out of bed and make an appearance at my real estate office. After throwing on a pair of jeans and a wrinkled blouse, I managed to drive to work. When I entered the building and passed my boss Jerry's private glassed cubicle on the way to my desk, I didn't stop to say hello. Two seconds later, his voice came over the intercom: "Amy Karl, please come and see me." I got up from my chair and sighed.

"Close the door," he said, as I walked in and took a seat opposite his desk. "What's going on? You look terrible."

Jerry was in his late sixties and always overdressed in his houndstooth blazers and ascot scarves. He had a poodle and lived with his boyfriend. He loved drama and was very blunt. Between sobs, I blurted out the whole sorry affair and breakup.

"Okay," he said. "From now on, you are only allowed to cry for ten minutes each day. Then you have to get on with it. That's always been my rule when I'm trying to get through something tough. Now go buy yourself a pair of sunglasses. It's not professional to show up to work with red, swollen eyes."

I promised him I would.

Later that night, as I sat in the tub, incapable of picking up a bar of soap to wash myself, I knew there had to be something else going on here. It wasn't normal to be this upset over someone I knew wasn't the one for me. Yet I felt so devastated. I realized—for the first time since losing my virginity, now many, many years ago—that as empowering as discovering my sexuality had been, great sex had also taken away my perspective about how ill-matched Matt and I were for each other. It had depleted me emotionally. This isn't to say there wasn't real value in discovering my g-spot. But I realized that sharing myself with someone so completely had left me feeling vulnerable and raw and utterly disposable. I was spent and tired and drinking two fishbowl-sized glasses of chardonnay every night to take off the edge. It was time to replenish my emotional bank account with something good and true to my heart. I wanted to start writing and acting again.

The following morning, I called a gal from my acting class who I thought was really talented and asked her if she wanted to help me write a short film spoofing Meg Ryan. She told me she was in, and we got to work on it right away. A few weeks later, we called USC Film School and had them post on their job board that we were looking for a director who would work for free in exchange for a reel for his resume. Two days later, we found our guy, and three days after that, we had a producer. Things were definitely looking up. Then a house sale I was counting on to fund the film fell through, and I couldn't afford to make it; and again, my tears were inexhaustible.

I called my doctor for advice, and he prescribed antidepressants. Between another relationship not working out, and my movie-making dreams being shattered, I felt I needed that little pill each day.

CHAKRA THREE

Oliver
April 2002 - August 2005

"Good things come to those who believe, better
things come to those who are patient, and the
best things come to those who don't give up."
—Anonymous

*I*ncreased suicidal thinking and behavior in children. *Abnormal ejaculating and gastrointestinal complaints such as constipation and flatulence. Nausea, vomiting, dry mouth, and anorexia. Dizziness, somnolence, abnormal dreams and sweating. Abnormalities of sex function. Insomnia, nervousness, and tremor. Cardiovascular effects such as hypertension.*

And finally... *yawning.*

I sat at the table and stared at the warning label on my bottle of antidepressants for several minutes. I could risk the anorexia and wasn't worried about premature ejaculation. But some of the others scared me. Approaching my thirty-third birthday, I rolled the small tablet in between my thumb and forefinger. *Was I really going to manage my problems with pills?* I come from a family of homeopaths. My great-grandmother on my mother's side was an artist who hung out with healers and cooked with all-natural ingredients. Growing up, my mom didn't allow me to pop a Motrin for my period cramps, which were excruciating. Until I was in college, I didn't know that two ibuprofen would give me back one day of my life every month. And all I could think about as I stared at my first tablet was that I hoped it would do the same: give me back the days I was losing being miserable. Picking up my glass of water from the table, I washed down my first capsule. Then I walked into the kitchen, opened the fridge, and poured a super-size-me glass of chardonnay. My doctor said it was okay.

That night, when I put my head on the pillow to go to sleep, I felt a hot tingling sensation inside my brain. I wondered if it was the dopamine already at work, firing through my synapses but decided that was a ridiculous thought. *It's only twenty-five milligrams*, I reminded myself.

One morning, I rolled over in my bed and opened the window. I was met with a pile of termite-infested wood that felt like fine sand. I reached for the small notebook on my nightstand and wrote on the top of the page in big capital letters: A1: CALL TO GET HOUSE TENTED. Since going on antidepressants a few weeks before, I was suddenly capable of making lists. I'm not talking just any old lists, either. I'm talking lists within lists. The kind you break down into A, B, and C categories and number 1, 2, and 3, in order to prioritize your day more efficiently. It was extraordinary that this was my new normal. Hopping out of bed, I quickly slipped into a sundress and drove to my office. I was the first one in for the fourth morning in a row. Heading to my desk, I passed Jerry's private cubicle.

"No more Chanel sunglasses?" he asked sarcastically as I breezed by him.

"Nope," I replied, taking a seat at my desk and opening my Rolodex to the place where I'd left off yesterday to roll calls to potential clients until lunch. For the remainder of the spring, this was my morning routine.

My company kept the "deal board" in the kitchen, so a lot of agents would pop in and out of this room throughout the day, pretending they wanted something to eat or drink. Really, they wanted to see who was up to what. In our office, the "deal board" was really the "ego board." It informed everyone just how productive each agent in our office had been all month. It never felt good if you didn't see your name on it.

One morning in June, after drinking another cup of H2O, I walked over to the board and wrote the address of my first new sale since going on anti-depressants in red magic marker.

"What did you sell?" a top-producing Realtor named Bill asked as he entered the kitchen. Bill was a real dynamo. I asked him if he ever saw the fixer upper in the Hollywood Hills that was practically falling off the cliff. He nodded that he had and told me what a tough sale that home was. Then he asked me how much I got it for. I told him close to full asking price. He nearly fell over.

"Who bought it?" he asked.

"Remember that Middle Eastern guy?"

"Mohamed finally bought something?" Bill asked in disbelief.

"He sure did. And I only had to show him a few things."

"You must be very effective," he said in a huffy tone before exiting the kitchen.

Mohammed had been Bill's buyer, but he could never get him to buy anything. So, allegedly, he'd let him go. I'd wanted to make sure I wasn't stepping on Bill's toes and asked him if he was okay with me representing Mohamed after meeting him at an open house, where he'd mentioned that Bill had shown him several properties. Bill's only advice to me was, "Stop wasting your time and go find a real buyer."

You must be very effective.

Yes, these antidepressants are definitely working, I thought. After just two months on Effexor, I was now the girl who could appreciate that little sliver of sunshine through my termite-infested bedroom window and sell Middle Eastern men cliffhangers at full price. I walked over to the water dispenser and gulped down my sixth glass of water like a nomad who'd been stuck in the Sahara for forty days. It helped me through my first side effect: constipation.

From the moment I moved to L.A., I had my heart set on living in this hacienda courtyard building on Laurel Avenue between Sunset and Fountain. I'd seen one of the bungalow apartments there when an old friend from college invited me over for tea right after moving to town. It was smack dab in the middle of West Hollywood, but it felt like it could have been in Tuscany. The entrance had a big wooden door with jasmine and bougainvillea running across the top and opened onto a magical courtyard where birds chirped, squirrels played, and fish jumped out of a koi pond.

The moment I walked in, I felt like I had entered the land of Oz. Everything on the outside of this door seemed dull in comparison. Between the pink roses, purple lavender, fragrant rosemary, and Japanese tree, I felt like Dorothy without the red shoes. *One day*, I'd said to myself.

That Saturday, with a hefty commission from closing on Mohammed's house just deposited, I drove past the building and saw the gardener sticking a For Rent sign in the ground with his foot. I rolled down my car window.

"Take that down," I said, jumping out of the car.

"*Que?*" he asked with a confused look.

"It's rented," I said with a smile, jotting down the landlord's number on my hand with a pen and stuffing the sign in my trunk before driving away.

A week later, I was in the courtyard, handing over a check to the property manager for my first and last month's deposit on the same top floor unit I'd had tea in and could never afford.

"Amy?" a gorgeous girl said, exiting her ground floor unit. It was the actress who had starred in that small movie I'd acted in a couple of years ago.

"Hey, Amanda," I said coolly. I could tell she was taken aback because actresses are used to everyone falling all over them, but I learned the minute you don't give actresses the attention they're accustomed to, they like you. Sure enough, there was a knock on my door later that night.

"Come in!" I yelled from my kitchen, which opened to the living room and entry. My new pied-à-terre was only a thousand square feet.

"Amy?" Amanda said, as she stepped inside, holding a pile of clothes.

"Hey, Amanda, what's up?" I asked in a cool tone.

"I thought you might like some of this stuff I got from various designers. The pants by Chloe are especially cute and I already have four pairs."

Actresses are always getting free clothes from designers. So, as I would soon discover, one of the perks about being friends with them is the hand-me-downs they pass on to you. Still, it wasn't lost on me that Amanda could have passed the hand-me-downs on to a lot of other people.

"Whatever you don't like, you can give back to me," she said, with the most fetching smile I had ever seen in my life. It was just bewitching, really. And, in that moment, I knew we would be friendly neighbors.

Later that week, I became really friendly with two other girls who lived in my complex, too. Chrissie lived directly across the hall from me. She was really bubbly and from Chicago. At 5'10" and with dirty blonde hair that fell down to the middle of her back, she looked like a supermodel. Chloe, the other gal, lived downstairs. Like me, she was pursuing acting. She looked like Molly Simms and was really bohemian and into new age spirituality.

One afternoon, I heard her singing from the courtyard on the way to my mailbox and knocked on her door. She was sitting cross-legged on her floor rubbing big wood mala beads between her fingers, chanting. Some guy in an orange robe who looked more like an affected actor than a Buddhist monk with his perfectly messy blonde locks and toned arms was chanting *"On Nam-myoho-renge-kyo."* Chloe opened one eye and motioned with her head for me to sit down. I took a seat next to her and tried to follow along. At first, I felt silly but as the words settled in and rolled off my tongue, I felt the same way I did when I hit tennis balls, like the whole world melted away and I was just in the moment. I knew that very second I was going to love living here.

The rent on my new apartment was triple what I paid Annie. I was determined to keep the deals rolling in. One afternoon at the office, I came across this little booklet in the bottom of my desk drawer titled *How to be successful in real estate in 4 weeks or less.* My company had given it to me when I first started but I couldn't deal. I pulled it out and gave the pages a quick scan:

"Memorize MLS statistics." *Boring.*

"Complete first market study." *Boring.*

"Take a top agent to lunch." *Now, that could be fun.*

And it just so happened that the top agent worked for my company's Beverly Hills' office. Richard used to get his postcards in the mail when I lived with him and mentioned in passing that if he ever got into real estate, this was the guy he'd want to emulate. I immediately picked up the company directory and called his extension.

"Joe Brown's office," a woman's voice answered.

I got a little intimidated. In my naïveté, I thought Joe was going to pick up.

"Is Joe in?' I mumbled.

The woman asked me what it was regarding. I told her I was a new agent at our company's Pacific Design office and wanted to take Joe to lunch. She wondered if it was to discuss a buyer I might have for one of his many multi-million-dollar listings. I told her that I wanted to talk to him about his journey to success because I needed a mentor. The other line went silent.

"Hello?" I asked.

"How about 1:00 on Friday, June 7th?"

It was a month out, but I wasn't about to negotiate the date. Especially when I heard chuckling in the background. I politely thanked her and told her I'd be in touch about where to meet. The week of the lunch, Joe's office called to reschedule for the following week. Then when that day approached, his office called to reschedule again. After the second time, I started writing the date in my day timer in pencil, but when I called to confirm a place the third time, his assistant told me he'd meet me at Kate Mantilini's Diner.

The afternoon of the lunch, I waited by the host stand for over forty minutes. I thought Joe forgot and was about to leave when a guy decked out in a Prada suit and fancy shades strolled in. He looked super rich and very L.A.

"Joe?" I asked.

He nodded at me. It seemed like he had a lot on his mind. But when you sell a couple hundred million a year like him, you probably would. We were immediately escorted to a booth and sat down. Joe didn't have a salesperson personality. He was quiet. When I started asking him questions about his career and real estate, he answered them in five words or less. The conversation was like pulling teeth. After placing our order, I knew this whole lunch thing was a wash and just decided to take off the real estate hat.

"Did you watch *Sex and the City* last night?" I asked.

"Oh my God, I can't believe Carrie got dumped in a Post-It!" he said. "My boyfriend and I were dying."

"Yeah, there's low and then there's really low," I said.

And so it went for the next twenty minutes until, finally, Joe shared how he became successful in real estate and offered me tips. He suggested I send out no more than five hundred mailers a month to start and that I sit other agents' open houses to pick up clients and get my name out. "In all my years of being the number one agent, no one has ever asked me to mentor them. I took this lunch because I was impressed," he told me. Then he asked me if I wanted to sit his five-million-dollar listing in Bel Air that weekend. Of course, I told him yes.

Over the next couple of weeks, Joe offered different open houses to me and even invited me to a client dinner to learn more about the business. This built my confidence and led me to ask other agents if I could sit their listings. One Sunday, a couple months after taking Joe to lunch, I sat an open house for the managing broker in my office and met a nice couple who was looking to buy. I especially hit it off with the wife, who was a producer for the morning news, and gave her my card. A couple of days later, I received a call from Mia Lee, an anchorwoman she referred. Mia wondered if I could come take a look at her home that evening. She wanted to put it on the market.

I closed on Mia's house that October and decided to put some of the money from the commission aside to make my short film. Pilot season was approaching (the season actors audition for all the new television shows), so I had to land a theatrical agent. I thought showcasing my acting over fifteen minutes (the length of my short) of film seemed the best way to accomplish this and invited my crazy good photographer friend, Kat, to lunch.

Kat had a lot of success shooting national campaigns for Martha Stewart, Target, Shabby Chic, and Gap. Over the course of dessert, I asked her how work was going. To my surprise, she said she was ready for a new challenge and confided how she wanted to expand into commercials but needed to direct something to put on her reel first.

"You should direct my short film," I said, shoving a piece of cake in my mouth. I was trying to seem really nonchalant about it all. She was kind of big time in her field.

"Send it over," she said. "I'd love to read it."

A couple of days later, Kat called and told me she thought my script was really sweet and charming. She wanted to direct. The only challenge was that she was six months pregnant and the holidays were approaching, so we needed to shoot it within the next couple of months. I told her this was not a problem because I was on a deadline, too, with pilot season approaching in the spring. But when I hung up, my head was spinning. I had less than eight weeks to secure a cast and crew and equipment and locations, not to mention prepare myself for the role. I called some of my actor friends at Playhouse West. Each of them knew someone who knew someone. Several meetings and phone calls later, I found my producer. She was a no-nonsense woman in her twenties from Greece and told me she would line up all the technical people, like the cameraman, director of photography, and sound guy. I was on my way.

Sliding into the Chloe pants Amanda had given me, I heard the seams split around my ever-expanding buttocks. "So much for anorexia," I mumbled. I looked into the mirror and saw the sides of my stomach flowing over the waistband—getting them buttoned was about as likely as a day without barbeque in Texas. With each new ounce of motivation and laughter attained by popping a pill, I'd added an equal and unwelcomed ounce of blubber. Since going on anti-depressants, I had gained ten pounds. Throwing my bathrobe on over my half-dressed body, I stomped into the kitchen and grabbed my notebook off the counter. To my ongoing list, I added: A1, eliminate alcohol for six weeks. Then I wrote: A2, go to spin class. Just as I finished scribbling down my new goals, Amanda knocked on my door. "Want to come to my birthday party on Saturday night?" she asked.

How could I possibly go to a party and NOT drink? Just as bacon goes with eggs, drinking goes with socializing. Still, she was a movie star.

"I would love to!" I answered.

"That seat's taken," a guy with biceps the size of my face proclaimed.

There was no towel or gym bag holding this particular bike, but I wasn't about to argue with a man who could bench press me.

"No problem," I said, moving my towel over to the handlebars of the next bike down.

"That bike's taken, too," he said. "In fact, this whole row is already reserved."

I walked back to the second-to-last row and found a different bike. I was pretty intimidated by the number of people swarming into the room who looked like they were born to ride. Then, as I mounted my bike, I saw Ozzy Osbourne seated on the bike behind me and breathed a sigh of relief. He was wearing little blue specs and was slumped down over the handlebars. It looked like the mere act of breathing was difficult for him. *If he can get through this so can I.*

Clicking my spin shoes into the pedals, I settled into the saddle. The seat was too high and the handlebars were too low, but I didn't want to deal with it and just stayed put. A few moments later, Tevia, the spin instructor, walked onto the stage where a single bike was mounted in front of the room.

"Ready to ride?" she hollered.

The whole room erupted in whistles as the first song blared over the loud speakers and everyone got out of their saddles and began pedaling to the beat of the music.

"Just follow the rhythm," Tevia said.

Although naturally athletic and coordinated, I was lazy when it came to playing sports. I just didn't have the drive to reach for that impossible shot on the tennis court or keep up with my mom when we went jogging. I never fully understood what athletes meant when they said they were "getting into the zone."

"One... two... three. One... two... three," Tevia counted through her headset.

It felt like she was talking to me, so I looked up from my bike. Sure enough, she was staring at me. Trying to pick up speed, my arms started shaking beyond belief and my legs felt like elastic. *What does she want from me?* I have never been blessed with rhythm—my sister teased me whenever we were on the dance floor together—so trying to find it under such difficult circumstances was beyond overwhelming. "One, two, three. One, two, three," I silently repeated, concentrating hard.

"That's it," Tevia said, flashing me a wink.

It was so annoying to be pushed like this at my very first class. But, at the same time, it felt good to win her approval. I could tell everyone here wanted to be the teacher's pet. "White Horses" began to play over the speakers. I followed the class back into the saddle. The song's beat was much slower than the previous one, so with the new verse Tevia instructed us to add resistance to the bike until it felt like we were climbing the highest hill in the world. Allowing the sound of the music to transport me to another place in my mind, suddenly I was on a sandy beach, drinking a margarita in a bikini with perfect abs. I wondered where Ozzy had gone in his head to ride Mount Kilimanjaro.

Over the next three minutes, no matter how physically exhausted I felt, I didn't lose my rhythm and kept up with all the little Lance Armstrongs in that class. Feeling high as a kite, I realized, for the first time, I must be "in the zone." My mind took me back to that night at Richard's when I got into downward dog. Something inside me knew it was time to revisit that transcendent pose that had helped put me back together again. On my way out, I grabbed a schedule off the front desk. There was a new yoga class on Wednesday mornings in studio B.

Of course, one spin class hadn't gotten me back into my skinny jeans, and I'd refused to go shopping for fat clothes. Sifting through my closet on the night of Amanda's party, my best option was a black raincoat that had a classic Audrey Hepburn vibe. I pulled it off the hanger and threw it over my big cashmere sweater and leggings. The raincoat would pass off as a chic winter pea.

A screenwriter friend of Amanda's was hosting her birthday at his apartment. He lived in a pre-war style building just a block up from my house, so I walked. No one ever walks anywhere in L.A. because it's too spread out. When I entered the lobby, I felt like I was in New York, with all the ornate moldings, crystal chandeliers, and wood paneling. A doorman in full uniform held a list.

"Name?" he asked.

"Amy Karl," I replied, as he consulted his clipboard with his index finger.

"Follow me," he said, crossing me off the list and escorting me up a small, wood elevator that opened into the apartment.

The room was packed with Hollywood hipsters, dripping in Marc Jacobs. I straightened my coat and discreetly dabbed some gloss on my lips, before weaving through the crowd. I recognized a few actors and agents, but I didn't see Amanda. I headed toward the dining room, where the bar was set up on a long wooden table. It was stocked with Grey Goose, Makers Mark, and every kind of chardonnay known to man. I spotted a bottle of seltzer water in the far corner and reached across the table for it. The bottle hadn't been opened yet so I tried to untwist the cap. It was on so tight I couldn't get it off. I brought the bottle in to the left side of my body for support and put all my strength into it. This time, the cap erupted off the bottle like a volcano on crack. A sea of bubbles began spraying all over the ceiling and me. I covered the top with my hand but the carbonation was too strong. The water squirted through my fingers all over my arms.

"Good thing you wore your raincoat," a guy's voice wafted over.

Looking up, across the table, I saw a very tall guy peering down at me over his glasses. He had a big toothy smile and disheveled salt and pepper hair. He looked like a big Saint Bernard and had the vibe of an absent-minded professor. I felt the heat rush to my face, unsure whether I was more embarrassed that my raincoat didn't come off as the winter pea I'd hoped it would, or impressed that he knew the difference. Rushing back to the living room, I spotted a couple of girls I knew sitting on the couch and sat down next to them. I still hadn't seen Amanda.

About twenty minutes later, I noticed Saint Bernard Boy in the far corner, staring me down with a couple of guys. One of them was a writer Amanda had just started dating. I instinctively pulled my sweater a little tighter across my chest. Amanda walked up. She seemed really tipsy.

"Happy birthday!" I exclaimed, standing up to hug her.

"Hey, see that tall guy over there in the glasses?" she slurred.

See him? I thought. *I just put him through a tsunami.*

"Yeah," I replied.

"His name is Oliver. He's a manager in town. Are you interested?"

Agents and managers are brilliantly gifted at planting seeds of insecurity in struggling actresses. I don't think they are intentionally trying to be unsupportive. I just think they witness firsthand how hard it is to make it as an actress, and they love to share these statistics with anyone trying to act, making it extra challenging to stay inspired and faithful to your goals. I was two weeks away from shooting my short film. I had to stay focused.

"I'm not really dating right now," I said.

"Okay," Amanda replied.

The week before the shoot, I ran around like crazy getting permits and insurance on all the locations we secured, getting the actors sign off on the required contracts from SAG, finalizing wardrobe, and practicing my lines. I was the most nervous about reenacting Meg Ryan's fake orgasm scene from *When Harry met Sally*. That whole week, I practiced every "Oh," and "Ah," and "Ewe" that she had uttered in the film, sitting on my bed. One night, I forgot to close my windows. The next day, I noticed that none of my neighbors could look at me. I didn't have a clue what was going on until my property manager, Alfonso, a gay Latin man with a passion for practicing his salsa routine, strutted into the courtyard in his tap shoes and black leather pants. "Someone's having fun up there," he said in his Spanish accent. "*Ew, ah, oh, ahhh.*"

"It's not what you think!" I shot back. "I was working on an audition."

"Whatever you say," he winked, before strutting off.

I was so embarrassed. I wanted to die. Instead, I drove over to Kat's house in Laurel Canyon. She was having the whole cast over to her place for a wardrobe fitting. A girl named Gaby who had worked on several of Kat's magazine shoots agreed to style the film for us. She was very New York: Thin. Direct.

"What size are you?" she asked one of the gals I had cast as one of the waitresses in my film.

The whole room stopped talking. This girl was at least a hundred pounds overweight.

"Extra large," the girl said.

Meanwhile, I struggled to zip up the side of a dress I'd be wearing for the ballroom scene.

"Do I look fat?" I asked Kat.

"You may want to drop five," she said before walking off.

Ouch. Even for the homemade movies, Hollywood could be so harsh.

We were scheduled to shoot the last Friday in January. We allocated three nights for the shoot which meant we had to shoot five pages a day. Each page is the equivalent of one minute of screen time. A blockbuster usually shoots 1.3 pages a day over a ninety-day period. We didn't have this luxury. Kat was now eight months pregnant and we were on a tight budget.

The first night we shot in a big warehouse we had rented out for the ballroom scene. Kat had some really lofty ideas of how she was going to create this environment. She hired a crane operator to swoop the camera down from the ceiling to the floor and a construction man to build some sets. When I walked into my first shot that Friday night and the camera came swooping down to my face from thirty feet above, I felt like a real movie star.

The second two days took place in a diner in Culver City. We had to go through all this red tape to get permits from the city and paid the owner eight hundred dollars a night to use the space from 3:00 p.m. to 3:00 a.m. It was really tricky, but we pulled it off, which wasn't easy considering the director of photography was a real diva and almost quit four times. He acted like he was working on *Titanic*, which secretly made me feel really special. "Cut!" he'd yell. "Let's change the lighting for the tighter angle." About halfway through the night, I saw Kat grab her lower back. She sat down on the stool and took a deep breath. I ran over.

"Are you going into contractions?" I asked. I was really worried, but she got right up and stretched her back.

"No, but we need to shoot this last indoor scene. The sun's going to be up in an hour," she said, pressing deep into her rib cage before limping off.

With fifteen crew people and extras hanging out waiting for me to perform my climax, I couldn't look at anyone. I just let it rip, from my deepest, darkest fantasy, before going quiet and taking a bite of apple pie with a big smile.

"And cut!" Kat yelled victoriously. Then she shot me a very approving wink. "That's a wrap," she said.

The following morning, I woke up feeling a sense of accomplishment I had never experienced before. I had finally taken matters into my own hands with my acting, applying everything I'd learned since moving to California and dumping it into my short. Throughout the day, several of the cast and crew called to thank me and congratulated me on a job well done, and I received flowers from my mom. Then Kat called.

"I woke up in a panic in the middle of the night," she said. "I think I forgot to shoot an important transition scene."

"We'll figure it out in the editing room," I said.

"Okay," she said, breathing a sigh of relief.

My response shocked even me. But suddenly the outcome of this little movie was less important to me than the fact that I had seen something through. This time, external forces could not transcend the internal sense of self. I felt like I'd won an Academy Award.

Later that afternoon, I saw Amanda in the courtyard for the first time since her birthday party. She asked me if I wanted to join her and a group of friends for dinner at the Chateau Marmont the following night. Oliver had asked her to extend the invite to me. I told her I'd be coming from my editing session in Santa Monica but as long as it was okay if I was a little late, I would come. She winked. "I'll save you a seat next to me," she said before fluttering off.

The following night, my phone rang during the editing session. I picked it up without looking at who was calling.

"Are you coming?" Amanda asked sweetly.

"Oh my God!" I proclaimed in horror. "I totally spaced!"

I looked at my watch. It was 9:30 p.m. I felt so rude and apologized profusely. But Amanda just chuckled and told me not to worry about it. Then, in a low whisper, she said, "I can tell Oliver is a little disappointed. Can I just give him your number?"

I told her yes, more out of guilt than anything else.

Over the next five days, I watched an editor into the wee hours of the morning (the moonlighting hours for people on a budget) run each frame of my film through a color-corrective process called Telecine. I didn't really need to be there, but I had invested enough of my own money that I figured I might as well learn everything I could about the post-production filmmaking process. The other reason I was willing to watch an editor until three in the morning, though, was vanity: The right color adjustments made to each frame of my face really helped me look younger and pop off the screen. It was my place to say "add a little more yellow" or "take down the blue" kind of thing. Needless to say, by the end of that week I was exhausted from pulling all-nighters.

That Friday afternoon, I fell asleep on my bed, a puddle of drool next to my mouth on the pillow. I had a greasy ponytail slapped atop my head because I hadn't showered for a couple of days. My phone rang, startling me awake.

"Amy? This is Oliver Kasey. I met you at Amanda's birthday party a few weeks ago."

Silence.

"Hello?" he inquired.

"I'm here," I replied, propping myself up onto my elbow, as I adjusted my eyes to the setting sun filtering through my blinds.

"I was wondering if you wanted to grab some sushi tonight?" he asked.

I think one of a man's great passions in life is, not a woman, but the challenge of getting a woman. *Why else would Oliver be so keen to go on a date with me?* I could hear Oliver's fingers returning emails through the phone in the background as he waited for my response. *A true multi-tasker*, I thought. I told him tonight wouldn't work.

"Come on. It's a really lowkey place. I can pick you up in forty-five minutes," he said.

"I won't be able to take a shower for you on such short notice," I said.

"Fair enough," he chuckled. "Where do you live?"

I gave him my address.

"We're neighbors!" he shouted jovially. "I just live a couple of buildings up."

L.A. is a very spread out city, so this is a very big deal. Traveling just three miles on the freeway can take one over an hour in traffic. I had a feeling that the convenience factor was a big point in my favor.

The minute I saw Oliver, I immediately wished I had washed my hair. He was much cuter than I remembered him sober on seltzer water. Maybe I was too preoccupied with shooting my short film to really see him before now. Plus, there was something about him that made me want to laugh. He had a befuddled quality about him, like he wasn't quite sure where he was.

I hopped into his car and thanked him for picking me up. He smiled and said it was not a problem as he drove two hundred yards up my street and pointed to a building.

"That's where I live," he said.

As soon as we arrived at the restaurant, I excused myself to go to the bathroom and tried to do something with my greasy ponytail. But this only made a bad situation worse, so I looked into the mirror and took a deep breath. Then I tightened my ponytail, pulled a little hair up at my crown to give my roots a much-needed lift, and walked out of the bathroom to go meet Oliver at the table.

A waiter came over and asked what we wanted to drink. I ordered seltzer water. Oliver told him he'd take a Sapporo, using the same smile he had when he picked me up. I almost felt the need to lick his face to wipe it off. For some reason, it just reminded me of the way a Saint Bernard would smile if a Saint Bernard were human, sort of big and wet and sloppy.

Within five minutes, three people stopped by our table to say hello to Oliver. One guy had an idea he wanted to pitch. Another had a script he was ready to submit. And the third had some notes on a current project. I realized he was sort of a big deal. I wondered if his perma-grin was some kind of coping mechanism to get him through the never-ending demands of his job.

Over the next hour, I learned that Oliver's firm represented actors and writers in Beverly Hills. Amanda and her boyfriend Josh were just two of the many A-listers he knew. Of course, I'd already learned from dating Richard that this didn't mean diddlysquat for me. I didn't need some jaded manager discrediting my low-budget short because he was producing an Academy-Award winning movie. At the same time, since going on antidepressants I was in a much better place than I was with Richard. I felt a chill of excitement as the night progressed. How could I have almost screwed this up? Then three words flew out of his mouth.

"I can't commit," he said.

Flagging down the waiter for a glass of chardonnay (three weeks shy of my six-week "no drinking" commitment), I felt anything but unflappable. Still, I looked him in the eye. "No problem," I replied with a chuckle. "You just hadn't met me yet."

"Well… I hope that's true," Oliver laughed.

Without realizing it on a conscious level yet, I had taken on a challenge much bigger than selling a cliffhanger, lunching a top Realtor, and completing my short film. I'd taken on the challenge to change a guy.

"Would you ever be interested in auditioning for a reality show that's equivalent to *The Bachelorette?*" Tevia asked me the following morning after spin class.

"Yeah, right," I laughed, dripping with perspiration.

She told me she was serious and that her friend Joe was producing a new show for NBC. She said that he had spun next to me a couple of times and asked her to ask me if I might be interested in auditioning. She told me it was supposed to be the competitor to ABC's *The Bachelorette* and that the first episode was scheduled to air that spring.

"So, let me get this straight. I could potentially be the equivalent to the next Bachelorette?"

"Yeah," she replied.

"Sounds like a disaster," I said.

"Why? Maybe you'll meet some really tall, handsome man."

"I think I already have," I gushed.

"Well, you don't have a ring on your finger yet," she said.

She did have a point. After a guy you've developed a crush on tells you he can't commit, I don't think there could be anything better than having a friend approach you about being on a network show that would provide you with twenty guys who could. Still, my instinct was to decline. People who aired their romantic laundry on reality shows were of a special breed. Even my parents, who perhaps suspected that life as an actress in L.A. could lead to this sort of opportunity, warned me if I ever chose to do a reality show that involved them, I'd have to hire a make-believe family.

"So what do you think?" Tevia asked again. "Can I just give Joe your email?"

Don't do it, Amy. Don't do it.

"I guess there's no harm in emailing," I replied.

Two days later, I threw on my most flattering sundress and headed over to NBC for my first interview. I was told I'd be meeting with the associate producer, not Tevia's friend Joe, who was a more senior executive on the show. A young male intern escorted me down a long, narrow hallway and into a small, stark room that looked like it was used for interrogating people. A single metal chair sat by itself in the middle of the room behind a line of tape, facing a single camera on a tripod. "Have a seat," he instructed.

As the back of my legs met the cold metal chair, sending shivers up and down my spine, a tall lanky man with big white teeth and shiny, tanned skin entered the room. His glow was more manufactured-looking than healthy. And I couldn't help but wonder if this show was his last chance at making it in the big time, perhaps allowing him to get some color in the south of France versus a tanning bed on Hollywood Boulevard.

"So what do you do, Amy?" he asked, turning the camera on me.

I knew from living in LA that reality TV pretended to want "real people," not actresses. I decided that I might as well wear the hat that could benefit me.

"I sell real estate."

"Really? Where?" he inquired.

"Prudential John Arroe & Associates," I answered.

"It's true!" the young intern, whom I didn't even know was still in the room, shot up from behind a curtain in the far corner. Apparently, he was fact-checking my answers from his laptop and had just pulled up my real estate website.

"We'd like you to go on to round two," the assistant producer said. He seemed really impressed that I had told the truth.

"What does round two consist of?" I asked.

"Oh, just a psychological test," he said.

"Okay," I replied, with a little too much enthusiasm for a girl who was telling herself she'd never do a reality show. Approval just felt too good to pass up.

A couple of nights later, I sat across from Oliver and smiled. It was our second date, and we were in the lobby of Chateau Marmont. Oliver was sitting in an old wing chair, and I was on a Victorian couch across from him, sipping on a glass of wine. I felt like I had a dirty little secret I wanted to divulge.

"How would you advise me if I were your client and asked if I should be the next Bachelorette?" I asked.

Without missing a beat, Oliver picked up his drink, cocked his chin down, and peered at me from over his glasses. "That it would ruin your life if you did it," he replied.

Like being an extra, doing a reality show was not good for an actress who wanted to be taken seriously. Even if I was going about the whole acting thing quietly at this point, I still wanted to be taken seriously. It had been painful being so close to people who could change everything for me, yet nothing ever changed. It was as if I was enough of an equal to be a *part* of their lives, but not enough of an equal to *live* their lives. A few seconds later, aloof Oliver got up from his chair and scooted next to me on the couch until we were shoulder to shoulder.

"Let's get out of here," he said, taking my hand in his and giving it a gentle tickle. He was so quirky.

"Sure," I smiled.

Like me, Oliver lived in a courtyard building with an Old World feel. Italian statues were scattered throughout mature landscaping and patina concrete slabs. Koi combed the surface of ponds with lips puckered for food. His apartment was charming with dark hardwood floors, high ceilings, and crown moldings; but it reflected his bachelorhood, too. His TV sat on the floor in front of a couch; his paintings were all stacked up against each other and leaning against the wall; and he had no light in the living room. *Nothing I can't help him with*, I thought as we walked over to the Brenda Antin couch, sat down, and looked each other in the eyes.

Oliver brought his hand to my face and delicately outlined my eye sockets with his fingers for several minutes. An issue of *Details* magazine lay on his coffee table. I wondered if the featured article this month proclaimed eye-socket outlining as some new kind of foreplay, or if this was just Oliver's idea of taking it slowly. Then, out of nowhere, he yanked my hair really hard.

"Ouch!" I yelped, as my neck snapped backwards.

"It's okay," he said, delicately outlining my lips with his fingers.

It was kind of erotic. The gentle act of tickling followed by the pull certainly wasn't what I expected. I was desperate to feel his lips as he leaned in and gave me a rather lovely and passionate kiss.

"That was nice," he said.

"Yes, it was."

I was definitely smitten.

Over the next two weeks, Oliver and I saw each other two nights a week. Unlike Matt, he had pretty defined boundaries, so I resolved myself to keep my boundaries in check, too, and continued talks with NBC in private. The possibility of meeting forty gorgeous men on national television was a good distraction from wondering where things would go with Oliver and seemed like a smart door to leave open. *Why put all my eggs in one basket?*

A couple of days later, the producer called and said I had made it to the next round. He told me this round consisted of meeting with the network's in-house psychiatrist and having a gynecological examination and series of blood tests to make sure I didn't have HIV or any other dating-deterrent diseases. He said the whole thing would take about two hours. That Wednesday, I headed to an urgent care center in Burbank and had my exam. Then I was told to go across the street to the Holiday Inn to meet the shrink. A young woman escorted me to a big table in the ballroom. She handed me a pen and thick stack of paper. "If you pass the written examination, you'll go on to meet the doctor," she said before leaving.

Suddenly, I got a little nervous. I hated tests. Then I read the first question: *If you worked for a restaurant and didn't think your minimum wage salary was fair, would it be okay to steal cash from the register when the manager wasn't looking? Circle Yes or No.* Twenty minutes later, the woman came back in and graded my test.

"Are there actually people who don't get a hundred percent of the answers right on this?" I asked.

"Oh, you'd be surprised," she said. Then she informed me that I hadn't missed any and was good to go meet the doc. I followed her up the elevator to the fourth floor. When we reached room number 33, she knocked on the door. "Good luck," she said before turning to go.

Besides a bad comb-over, the doctor was charming and affable. He asked me a series of questions about dating.

"Have you ever shown up unannounced to an ex-boyfriend's house when you found out he was dating someone new and thrown a fit?"

"What do you think about a woman who slits the car tires of an ex because he broke up with her?"

"Have you ever followed your ex across town in your car?"

Essentially, they were questions that could only flag me if I'd answered "yes" to *"Would it be okay to steal cash from the register?"*

On the way home, I called Sloan. "I passed with flying colors."

"Oh, Blooper," she said, "this is all so exciting! You are going to be the next Trista! I will call you later." *Click.*

There was still a lot of post-production work to do on my short film. I had to find an editor to cut and paste it all together, a composer to write the score, and a sound guy to lay the score over the final picture. As fate would have it, an actor in my class referred me to an editor friend of his looking to buy a condo in the Valley. I usually didn't sell condos in the Valley, but I told this buyer I'd be willing to find him a place and pay for his inspection if he'd give me a huge break on his editing services. He agreed. A few weeks later, I had another sale under my belt and a very rough cut of my movie to show Kat. "I guess some things can't be fixed in the editing room," Kat said, her new baby boy wrapped in a sling across her chest. "But I have an idea."

That Thursday I was back in costume, being filmed getting in and out of a rented limousine parked in Kat's driveway while a few of our friends snapped flash until I was blinded and Kat said, "That should do it!"

The head producer of the reality show called and told me that it was down to me and one other girl.

He asked me to meet him at the studio commissary that afternoon. When I arrived, a clean-cut looking man in his forties approached me at the vending machines. He told me he was the head producer and escorted me to a corner table. He was clutching a black binder. "You're runner up," he said, before I even had a chance to take my purse off my shoulder and sit down.

"Okay," I replied, trying hard not to sound defensive or disappointed.

He opened the black binder he was holding. It was filled with pictures of unattractive, odd-looking men. "These are the guys you would have been set up with," he told me, pointing to a Caucasian man who was all of three feet tall, then to a bald African-American who had to be eight-foot-two. I thought he was on stilts until I saw his eighteen-inch tennis shoe on the ground.

"The show's concept is a pretty girl who has to endure dates with misfits, midgets, and nerds," he said, leaning in. "It's called *Average Joe*," he whispered, pushing a confidentiality agreement in front of me to sign. "But you can't tell anyone. So, what do you think?"

I was appalled that I had invested this much time in auditioning for a show I was led to believe was the equivalent of ABC's *The Bachelorette*. But more than that, I was humiliated that I had just been informed I wasn't good enough. I had come in second to some Miss America contestant with a much better body.

"I think it's very cruel," I replied.

"Really?" he said, gathering his binder.

"Yes, really," I replied, as he waved the confidentiality agreement in my face with a peculiar look in his eye, thanked me for coming, and left.

A few moments later, a junior assistant escorted me to my car in the parking lot. I felt like I had been sucker punched in the gut. Luckily, I was having dinner with Oliver at seven. Maybe I would show him my rough cut of *When Katie Met Meg*. He'd been begging me to see it, and after this debacle, I could really use the encouragement. Plus, I needed an agent. My movie was behind schedule. It was already April. Pilot season had already begun.

"In the kitchen!" Oliver yelled.

I let myself into his apartment and walked back. Oliver was pulling salmon out of the broiler and steaming Brussels sprouts.

"You're such a healthy eater."

"Lack of vitamin E makes the feet smell," he said.

I snorted. He was so quirky. I loved that about him. I also loved that he had set the dining room table. Not wanting to let on that I hated salmon, I washed down every bite with my water when Oliver wasn't looking. After my day, I was craving comfort food, like mashed potatoes.

"I found out I was the runner up for the Bachelorette show."

"Are you okay with that?' he asked.

"I sort of already like a guy."

Oliver flashed me a huge toothy smile. "Good to know," he said.

After dinner, I drummed up the courage to pull out a DVD from my purse. "So I have a very rough cut of my short." Oliver grabbed the disk out of my hand and turned on his TV. He seemed genuinely excited to watch it. I couldn't bring myself to look at the screen and kept my eyes on Oliver. To my delight, he had a perma-grin on his face every time I was on the screen. He laughed at the orgasm scene, lit up when my character lost her shoe, and smiled as I was reunited with my Prince Charming. But when the movie was over, he didn't say much or offer to show it to anyone, forcing my hand.

"So, what did you think?" I asked.

"Your acting was really good. But I just don't handle this kind of stuff."

Although, technically, Oliver only managed writers, his company worked with lots of actors, and he was one of the owner/partners. It really hurt to hear.

"Well, thanks for letting me show it to you," I said.

"Of course. Of course," he said in a very affable tone.

The following day, I asked Amanda if she would take a look at my short. She told me of course and ran up to my apartment. "Have you shown this to Oliver?" she asked. "You should." I told her I had but that he said he didn't really know what he could do with it. She shot me a funny look, like she didn't buy it, but I didn't press her on the subject. Oliver worked with A-list actors like Amanda, who was in the middle of shooting *Something's Gotta Give* with

Jack Nicholson. So I felt a little stupid talking any more about my homemade movie.

I was scared. I had reached a plateau with my anti-depressants. They were no longer keeping me happy like they once did at my current dosage of seventy-five milligrams because my body had grown accustomed. Emptiness and despair were resurfacing. I called my doctor and told him I didn't think the Effexor was working anymore. He asked me to remind him what dosage I was taking. I told him seventy-five milligrams. "That's not very much. A hundred and fifty milligrams should "jump-start' your joy," he said.

But then what would it be? I wondered, because surely, like the drug addict graduating from pot to cocaine to heroin, I, too, would need to graduate to new levels of intake in order to keep the happy high going. And what effect would one hundred fifty, three hundred fifty, or six hundred milligrams of Effexor have on me?

Later that week, I was at Oliver's house. We were sprawled out on opposite ends of the couch watching TV together. My feet were in his lap.

"Do you feel that?" he said.

"Feel what?" I asked.

"Your foot's tremoring," he said. "It happens all the time, starts shaking like that. Can't you feel it?" he inquired off my confused look.

Excusing myself to the bathroom, I pulled my Effexor out of my purse. I remembered that neurological ticks were a side effect but didn't see anything on the bottle. The following morning, I called my doctor again and told him about the tremor and suggested that perhaps it was time to wean myself off the medication. "I wouldn't recommend that," he said. I asked him why. "I want you to get used to wearing the happy hat just a little longer."

I decided to take his advice. But when I popped my pill that day it wasn't lost on me that every time I swallowed it, I was, on some subconscious level, telling my mind and body that it was filling a hole in me. Antidepressants reinforced in me this belief that I needed to take medication to feel good in my life. In this moment, I opened myself up to the idea that perhaps I could also fill this dark hole—the one where emptiness, loneliness, and despair resided —organically.

That Wednesday, I headed to Body and Soul for a yoga class I had seen on the schedule. I had still only done yoga a dozen or so times. When I walked into class a drop-dead gorgeous blonde sporting cleavage was singing along to The Rolling Stones' "Beast of Burden" blasting from her CD player in the front of the room. I looked around to make sure I was in the right place. I was ten minutes late and no one else was there.

"Welcome. I'm Lulu," she whispered, quickly switching the song on her CD player over to a mantra being sung in Sanskrit, which I didn't know was Sanskrit yet because I'd never heard the language before. "I think it's just going to be you and me today," she continued with a smile. "Would you like to do a set that brings in opportunity?"

I had no idea what this chick was talking about. Wasn't yoga about tying your body into a pretzel? But her energy was different from all the other people I'd come across in this gym. She seemed to have a white light glowing around her body as if she'd drunk a glass of sunshine.

"Opportunity sounds good," I said, rolling my mat out in front of her and getting into a cross-legged position.

Lulu suggested a set for the heart center, explaining that when the heart is open, opportunity can come in with more ease. Then she spread her perfectly toned arms out like the wings of an angel and brought her hands into a prayer pose in front of her chest. *Is this chick for real?* I wondered, obediently following suit.

As I rubbed my palms together like she did, I felt of a surge of energy rise up my spine. I hadn't felt anything like it since Matt. I closed my eyes and took a deep breath from my navel. I felt immediately connected to myself. And at some point it occurred to me that it was my own hands, not the hands of some guy, activating it. I flexed my spine, rotated my wrists, and did circle eights with my neck to the sound of my breath. I felt transported to someplace beyond me. Unfortunately (or fortunately, depending on how you look at it), over the next four weeks I was the only one who showed up to class, so Lulu told me it was going to be pulled from the schedule. Kundalini yoga has nothing to do with sculpting your body and everything to do with sculpting your soul: a hard sell for a gym overpopulated with women spinning until their eyeballs popped out, wearing a size zero.

The last day of class, I asked Lulu if there were any other places in Los Angeles that taught Kundalini. She told me to check out this woman named Gurmukh at Golden Bridge Yoga Studio. She said she was one of the most renowned teachers on the continent for Kundalini yoga. I thanked her and embraced her one final time.

In June, Oliver and I flew to San Francisco for the weekend to attend my friend Lila's wedding. We stayed at Ian Shrager's new hotel in Union Square. Oliver was obsessed with modern architecture, and the hotel had recently been renovated and got an honorable mention for its design.

"What time's the wedding again?" Oliver asked at check-in.

"Not until 5:30 tomorrow," I said, as the concierge passed me two hotel keys and informed us that the glow-in-the-dark condoms were in the dish next to the bed.

Even though Oliver and I were spending up to four nights a week together and not seeing anyone else, he wouldn't let his naked body get within a foot of me unless a condom was within an arm's reach. So this was a good perk. Our room was on the twelfth floor. It had a view of the Golden Gate

Bridge, a plasma TV, and, as promised, a dish stocked with an assortment of multi-colored condoms. It was totally swanky. Oliver pulled me into his arms and gave me a tender kiss.

Oliver and I never fought. He was easy and agreeable. He laughed at all my jokes, never told me what to do, and was very patient. I, on the other hand, had to make a conscious effort to be patient with him. Although he was on top of managing his clients' lives, he moved like a turtle when it came to his own. It took him two hours to take a shower and get dressed, an hour to make a salad, and five years to decide what kind of couch he'd like to buy. He was a case study in the exercise of patience.

After the rehearsal dinner that night, we met up in the hotel lobby for drinks with a couple of my college friends who lived in San Fran and hadn't been invited to the wedding. The place was packed, but there was only one guy to every ten women. One of the girls we were meeting always said San Francisco was a city with a shortage of men, and now I believed her.

Oliver and I meandered our way around several pieces of high velvet furniture until we reached the bar. My friends were already sitting at a table and had a round of drinks waiting. They were all really excited to meet Oliver, who flashed his infectious smile and offered to buy a round. About three drinks into the night, Oliver and I were holding hands, being all adoring of each other. My friend Sally smiled approvingly at us. "So how long have you guys been boyfriend and girlfriend?" she asked Oliver.

I felt Oliver's grip on my hand relax. We had the understanding that we were only seeing each other. Just a few weeks earlier, Oliver told me he didn't want me to date anyone else. So I'd never felt the need to ask the junior high question, "Do you want to be my boyfriend?" I assumed it was a given—but not Oliver, I guess. He was tongue-tied. I decided to help him out and looked at Sally. "About three months," I told her. Then I turned toward Oliver with an adoring fake smile. "Wouldn't you say that's about right?" I asked.

"Uh…. yeah, I guess so," he said sheepishly.

The whole mood around the table changed, and I felt really humiliated.

"Hey, you guys want another drink?" Sally asked, in an attempt to break the awkwardness. It was so obvious that she wanted to change the subject and make things better for me. But I just suggested we get the check.

After we paid the bill, I stormed to the elevator and then down the hallway to the room, at least three feet ahead of Oliver. The second he walked through the door, a look of dread was on his face.

"Mind telling me why that question was so painful for you?"

"I don't think we need to label us yet, that's all," he replied, looking down.

"You're pathetic," I said, slamming some things into my suitcase.

"I really adore you," he said, wrapping his arms around my waist from behind.

"Then I really don't get it," I said.

By the end of the night, Oliver acknowledged that hanging out four days a week for the last couple of months probably did, in fact, make us boyfriend and girlfriend. I knew we had moved to the next level. I also knew that if I wanted to be with Oliver, I had to be patient and trust him. Everyone—our friends, his colleagues—told me that he lit up whenever I walked into the room. Sloan even took it a step further and said, "But he'll be the last to know." Oliver always had a look on his face that suggested he was on the brink of some great discovery. And now that we had taken our relationship to the next level, I was hopeful his great discovery would be me. Even if he would be "the last to know."

The following morning, Oliver and I walked up to reception to check out of the hotel. A stunningly beautiful young woman in her early twenties stood at the front desk.

"Are you an actress?" Oliver inquired, as he signed the bill.

"No," she said, batting her eyes. "But I'd be open to trying."

"Now that's just the kind of girl my company would love to sign," Oliver whispered to me, as he stuffed his receipt in his jeans pocket and we headed toward valet.

It was like *déjà vu* all over again: I was reliving the Piper Perabo episode I went through with Richard years earlier when he told me his agency had signed her just for walking into the camera frame and saying nothing.

As we drove over the Oakland Bridge to the airport, I was really quiet. Oliver knew I had busted my butt to make my short film with the hope I would find someone to represent me or at least acknowledge me. I was hoping this person might be my boyfriend. But not once had Oliver ever offered to be this person or to have someone in his company be this person if it was too close to home for him. Perhaps Oliver and Richard were more alike than I thought.

Ironically, the Tuesday after I returned from San Francisco, I bumped into Richard (who, of course, was already in the top one percent of Realtors nationwide) at a brokers' open house I was previewing for a client in the Hollywood Hills.

"I hear you're dating Oliver Casey," he said. I told him it was true. "He's a great guy," he told me.

Later that night, I told Oliver I never realized he and Richard knew each other well enough for Richard to give him such an endorsement. Neither one of them had ever made reference of the other in front of me before. Oliver confided that Richard had really pushed for him to rent the extra bedroom in his house next to Mike, but that he wasn't into it. I told him that was probably good because otherwise we would have been roommates. I wanted to barf. Hollywood could be so incestuous. There was no escaping your past.

It was time to call the Golden Bridge to see when Gurmukh was teaching. I totally butchered her name. "Ger mook," the receptionist corrected me. When I walked into the studio the following afternoon, I was a little taken aback. All the male and female teachers were dressed in white long dresses called *kurtas* and wore head turbans. The men had long black-and-gray beards down to their chests. Although I knew Kundalini was a different form of yoga, I wasn't expecting the dress code to remind me—and I hate to say this because it makes me sound so ignorant of other cultures– of being in the Middle East. Lulu might have chanted things in Sanskrit, but she looked like the type of yoga instructor I'd grown accustomed to seeing on all the DVD jackets gracing Rodney Yee's videos while shopping at Whole Foods: black leggings, colorful tank tops. Still, I didn't let their dress code deter me. I knew these teachers represented love and peace and all that was still good about our planet. Sometimes, different just takes a little getting used to. I liked different.

On my way into the yoga room, a cute woman who reminded me of the fairy godmother from Cinderella stopped me. She was clearly a teacher, with her flowing white skirt and huge head turban. "Oh dear, you need some healing," she said. "You had too much sex with the wrong guy a while back and it took a lot out of you." Intrigued by her psychic ability, I told her she must be talking about Matt and introduced myself. She said her name was Tej and that I should come to her class on accessing intuition. Then she was off to help Gurmukh.

When I finally rolled out my mat and took a seat, I noticed that everyone but me was sitting on a sheepskin and was dressed in white leggings and t-shirts. Gurmukh was wearing a beautiful white dress with yellow embroidered sleeves. A pendant necklace made of amethyst was draped around her neck, and a gold gem was pinned in her turban above the third eye. She looked like a queen.

After we tuned in, she told us that Kundalini came from India to the U.S. in 1969. Until then, it had been under lock and key. Kundalini was a form of yoga reserved for the crème de la crème of yogis. She said it was like taking a jet instead of a car in terms of transformation (not transportation). It was *that* powerful. Then she instructed us to get into downward facing dog and to "hold it" for fifteen minutes. She said holding this pose for this amount of time could cure any disease. Although this sounded farfetched, I couldn't help but be transported back to Richard's bedroom three years earlier when I was so riddled with anxiety I thought I might die, until… I got into this exact same pose and everything settled, and I was once again at ease instead of dis-*ease*.

"Today, we will be doing a meditation for prosperity," Gurmukh said, as we held the posture. "Now this does not mean everyone will become rich," she continued, taking a dramatic pause as gasps of disappointment filled the room. "Sometimes, not being able to pay the rent is what transforms us. Sometimes, it's not until we are under all that pressure that we, like that piece of coal, can become a diamond."

Oliver had never dated anyone for longer than six months. So, privately, I was always preparing myself for our breakup in July. Instead, Oliver invited me to go to a wedding with him in August in Tuscany. The groom was a writer Oliver represented, and he was marrying into one of America's oldest families. The plan was to stop in Sienna first for a couple of days, then go to Florence for the wedding, then Positano for two nights.

In Sienna, we checked into an old hotel with cement walls, marble floors, and ivy-covered patios. It was off the main square, and our room had a large window with wood shutters that opened up to a view of green rolling hills and terracotta-colored rooftops. It was the perfect backdrop for romance and made me want to sing out loud to the birds.

The first night in the hotel, Oliver and I were lying naked underneath a white linen sheet. Oliver was on his back, his right leg hanging off the side of bed. I was lying on my stomach, enjoying the gentle breeze wafting through our open window. All was still and calm. Then I heard this little noise. Oliver sat up and screamed.

"A bat just flew into our room!"

"What!" I yelled, flipping myself onto my back and sitting up in fear.

"A bat!" he hollered, hopping up off the bed.

I expected him to swat it with a magazine or a towel. Instead, he ran into the bathroom and locked the door, leaving me alone in the room, as the wing expansion on this squawking beast took over the entire ceiling. I pulled the sheets over my head and started laughing.

"Where's my batman?" I screamed from under the covers, at the top of my lungs.

"In the bathtub!" he yelled.

"Pussy," I laughed.

I could hear Oliver laughing from the bathroom, which triggered hysterical giggles from me. Despite our laughter, though, I had this little feeling of dread. Oliver had just taken flight from me rather than fight for me. But I couldn't worry about this now. We were in Italy, for God's sake and, after a day of getting over our jet lag, Oliver and I managed to fall back into romance easily. We fed each other pizza, drank lots of delicious red wine, strolled hand in hand from piazza to piazza, and made sure to snuggle with the windows closed.

A large group of us from L.A. were staying at the same hotel in Florence. It didn't have the Old World charm of the place we stayed at in Sienna. It was hip and modern, like a W Hotel that could be in New York or Miami. But the windows didn't open, so there were no more bats to worry about.

The night of the wedding, a bus shuttled us up to an old brick estate with grapevine-covered walls. As Oliver and I were ushered to our seats, I took in all the blue bloods wearing bow ties in the front row and wondered how the girl who didn't know anyone out in California when opening that letter just five years ago got here. Just then, a woman wearing a turban approached the podium. I looked down at my wedding program to see who it might be.

"Gurmukh's officiating?" I blurted out in shock.

Oliver asked me who Gurmukh was. I told him she was a revered Kundalini yoga instructor back in L.A., and that I did her class once. Oliver wondered who names their kid Gurmukh. I told him it was a given spiritual name she received and translated to "one who lives and breathes words of divine wisdom and communicates that essence deeply from her heart." I had checked it out on her website. Still, I couldn't believe I remembered the meaning so distinctly. Although I had felt a little overwhelmed by the turbans and *kurtas*, here in Italy, Gurmukh inspired every part of me. "Isn't she beautiful?" I said to Oliver, halfway through the ceremony. He nodded.

After the vow exchange, I noticed Gurmukh sitting off by herself as all the guests drank champagne and scarfed down cheese and prosciutto. I couldn't have gotten near her if I had tried back in LA. Students swarmed around her after class, waiting their turn to get some piece of enlightened advice. But here in Tuscany, not many people knew who she was (yet). It felt disrespectful not to approach her.

"Gurmukh?" I said timidly.

"Yes," she offered warmly.

"My name's Amy. I took one of your classes back in L.A."

"You should take teacher's training with me this fall then."

"No, I think maybe you misunderstood. I'm not a teacher. I've only done Kundalini a few times."

"Well, you're the perfect candidate then. Becoming a teacher is how you find your way into the practice."

That December, Oliver invited me to the premiere of *Something's Gotta Give* and his company's Christmas party. This was a big step for Oliver. Unlike Richard, who included me in his whole life after our first date, Oliver was very guarded and protective about whom he let into his inner work circle. I thought it was a good sign that our relationship was progressing. We were at the nine-month mark of dating. Now, I just yearned for him to tell me he loved me.

The premiere was at the same theatre I'd dragged Sloan to in Westwood for *Cruel Intentions*, now three years ago. I thought it warranted a call to her as I was heading over and picked up the phone to tell her where I was going.

"My next goal is to hear those three little words," I said.

Sloan laughed. "Darling, EVERYONE knows he loves you. It's just…"

"He'll be the last to know," we shouted simultaneously.

Even though we shared a good laugh, her observation haunted me. I couldn't wait ten years for Oliver to figure things out. I was already thirty-four.

Oliver was coming from work so he instructed me to meet him in the lobby. I was really excited because Amanda was in the movie. She was bringing her boyfriend, the same guy she had just started dating around her birthday. He was an amazing writer who Oliver respected. When I strolled into the crowded lobby, I saw the three of them chatting and walked up. We exchanged kisses and hellos. Then everyone began to file into the theatre.

"So we'll see you after the movie?" Oliver turned to me and said.

"What?' I asked in confusion. I assumed we would all sit together.

"We already saw it. We're going to go grab a bite at Jerry's Deli next door."

"Well, I don't have to see the movie now. I'll come with you," I said.

"We're going to talk a little business. We'll come get you after," he said, giving me a kiss on the cheek.

I told him okay, but as I walked into the theatre all by myself, I didn't feel okay. I felt like an outsider. My eyes welled up with tears. When I walked into the lobby after the movie, Oliver, Amanda, and Josh were waiting for me.

"Awww," Amanda said, noticing my red, puffy eyes. "You liked it."

I could tell she was touched by the emotion she thought her movie had emitted from me and didn't want to ruin her moment.

"You were just great," I said. And I meant it. She really was good, and so was the movie.

That New Year's, I stood across from Oliver, who was seated on the edge of the bed. We were in Aspen with a group of people from Los Angeles. Chrissie was there with her boyfriend from New York. I held up my first flash card. "Repeat after me," I instructed.

> Me: I
>
> Oliver: I
>
> Me: Love
>
> Oliver: Love
>
> Me: You
>
> Oliver: You
>
> Me: Amy.
>
> Oliver: Amy.

"See, it's easy," I said, putting the cards down on the nightstand.

Oliver's face contorted into a look of pained confusion as he digested what I had just tricked him into. I watched him get up from the bed and walk into the bathroom to gargle. Even though I believed Oliver wanted my help in getting him over the "I love you" hump, the whole thing felt cringeworthy. Luckily, the subject didn't come up again that trip. Then, when we got back to L.A., something extraordinary happened: Oliver couldn't stop saying "I love you, Amy." It didn't matter where we were, what we were doing, or how many times he had already told me in a day. Within three weeks of returning from our Sesame-Street-flash-card-session in Aspen, it was as if Oliver had a bad case of obsessive-compulsive disorder:

> Oliver while reading a script in bed: Amy?
>
> Me: Yah, sweets?
>
> Oliver: I love you.
>
> Me: I love you, too.
>
> Oliver while turning the page of some other script the following day: Amy?
>
> Me: Uh-huh?
>
> Oliver: I love you with every bone in my body.
>
> Me: Awww. That's sweet. I love you with every bone in my body, too.
>
> Oliver getting up to take a bathroom break before reading Act Two: Amy?
>
> Me: Yes, I know you do, cutie. You don't have to tell me anymore today.

Although these words were comforting at first, it didn't take long for them to become annoying. As time went on, the milestones that usually accompany them were not being met: I still didn't have a key to his place; he rarely slept over at my house; and we never talked about our future. But then, one

Thursday night around this time, Oliver called out of the blue.

"Can I come over?" he asked. I nearly dropped the phone. Oliver always wanted me to go to his house. He never offered to come to mine. When he arrived, he looked a little tired and disheveled. I made him some dinner and asked him about his day. Nothing out of the ordinary had happened. I asked him what motivated him to come over on a work night.

"I realized there's no other place I wanted to be," he said, gently taking my hand in his. It was the most organic moment our relationship had ever had. Oliver may have had his quirks and been a slowpoke, but I was really falling for him.

That spring, I submitted my short to various film festivals around the country. It was a year later than I had hoped but, after many edits, it was the best it was going to be. The trend in shorts that season was a super edgy and dark storyline. Our film could have been a Disney movie. It was fluffy and light. Something you could definitely show your grandma. So, needless to say, it was rejection after rejection. Then Kat called. "We got into the Beverly Hills Film Festival," she said. I was ecstatic and asked her when it was. She told me the screening ran from May 6 through May 9 at the Clarity Theatre and was followed by an awards ceremony and dinner at The Beverly Hills Hotel on May 9. It sounded fancy.

After we hung up, I immediately called Oliver to share the news and asked him to be my date.

"When is it?" he asked.

I repeated the dates, but the other end of the line went silent.

"Hello?"

"I have to be in New York that weekend to check out Josh's set," he said.

I asked him if he could reschedule for the following weekend, but he told me no.

"I'm really sorry," he said.

Although I was disappointed, I got it. His job was his job. This client was an A-list writer. I would just go on without him. And I was kind of glad I did. The weekend of the festival was a little anti-climatic. Besides a few laughs and a cheer after the orgasm scene, we didn't win any awards and no agents were knocking on my door. Another pilot season came and went, leaving me no other choice but to chalk up the making of *When Katie Met Meg* as an incredible experience and shelve it.

That summer, I brought Oliver back to Chicago for the 4th of July. He had never been there. We spent a couple of days in the city, then we went up to my family's beach house near New Buffalo. I invited Annie and Polly to come, too. Oliver was on his phone the whole time we were in the city, but once we got to the beach, he really seemed to relax. We drank margaritas, walked the beach, and took the jet skis for a spin. On our last night, we were taking in the view of the sunset together, sitting on the sand, sipping on a glass of wine.

"Bubs," Oliver said. "I do love you with every bone in my body."

When we got back to L.A., it felt like the trip marked a new milestone in our relationship. We were closer than we'd ever been. One night in early October, Oliver and I were sitting on his couch reading the Sunday paper together. I was reading the style section and Oliver was scouring the real estate section. "I think it's time to buy a house," he said. I brought the paper down from my face and looked at him. "I'm serious," he continued.

Over the next three months, I showed Oliver every mid-century modern, craftsman, and Spanish that came on the market. There was one modern in the Hollywood Hills I thought Oliver was going to buy because he spent two hours there (the average showing is fifteen minutes) and went back four times. It had the pool, views, kitchen, and location Oliver said he wanted. Toward the end of the showing, we were sitting out on the patio taking in the sunset. I asked him if he wanted to make an offer. "No, I don't like the roof line," he said.

Next, there was the mid-century modern off of Woodrow Wilson. An important architect built the home, and the views of the valley were amazing. Unfortunately, the ceilings were too low for Oliver's six-foot-five frame, so after he walked into the kitchen for the third time and asked the listing agent his forty-fifth question, I said, "Time to go," and shuffled him out.

Finally, a little Spanish in the flats of Beverly Hills came up. Coincidentally, the listing agent was a woman Oliver knew from years back. When Oliver went to check out the backyard for a fourth time, I stayed behind in the living room and chatted her up. During the course of our conversation, it came out that she'd shown him over ten places months before we'd started dating.

"So, how are things going with you two?" she asked, all curious.

"Good, really good. I just wish I could find him a place already," I replied jokingly.

"Amy!" she said in a get-real-tone, looking me directly in the eye. "Do you know how long it took him to buy that club chair in his living room?'

"The red one with the thick arms?"

"That's it."

"How long?"

"Two years," she proclaimed. "And trust me, I should know. On the days we went house hunting, he must have dragged me to that furniture store on La Cienega at least three times. It was always the same thing. 'Are the lines clean?' 'Is the cushion too thick?' 'Does the leather look old enough?' I don't know how you do it."

"Oh, he's going to buy something," I said.

"Well, I hope that's true for your sake."

When Oliver came in from the backyard, I decided to put a little pressure on him. "So what do you think?'

"I like it," he said in a serious tone.

"Well, let's make an offer," I said.

"No. I don't like how the roof is pitched instead of flat in the back of the house," he replied, before turning to the other agent. "Do you have any mid-century moderns coming up?"

"You don't fit in those," I interrupted. They both looked at me in confusion. "The ceilings in all the mid-century homes in your price range are too low for your height, remember?"

"Oh yeah," Oliver chuckled with that infectious laugh that made us all laugh back. Yet, in this moment, I realized it was no longer the kind of laugh that took a load off. I felt exhausted by it.

That November, I found a great Spanish in the Hollywood Hills when I was out previewing homes on Tuesday's Broker caravan. It had the perfect combination of modern and Spanish. I immediately called Oliver. "Bring your checkbook!" I said. "I found the house you are going to buy."

"Really?" he said.

"You need to come see it, now."

A couple of hours later, we were in my car outside the house, discussing all its amazing features. After my nagging persistence, I handed him a pen and contract and watched him reluctantly sign the offer I had quickly filled out on my lap and shoved in his face before he could change his mind.

"I better not tell you to go save the world next," he chuckled. "You might go buy a suit of armor."

The following month, I rolled over in Oliver's bed and let out a frustrated huff, as I scratched a little more.

"Maybe it's dermatitis," he said with concern.

"Nope," I replied, itching the inside of my upper thighs with the abandon of a seven-year-old with chicken pox. "The dermatologist did a skin test already."

"Well, I wish there was something I could tell you."

"Me too," I replied, hopping off the bed and walking into the bathroom to apply more ointment and draw another oatmeal bath. I was on my eighth tube of cortisone and twenty-fourth pack of Aveeno bath salts.

Over the last couple of months, I'd developed a chronic itch around the outside of my privates that no doctor could diagnose. My gynecologist checked for yeast and diabetes; my internist drew my blood; and, my dermatologist ruled out psoriasis and dermatitis, leaving me close to tears. I told her I didn't know how many more oatmeal baths I could handle. "Have you thought about going on antidepressants?" she'd asked. I said I didn't understand the correlation, and she explained that an overreactive nervous system might be causing my itching. She told me that a recent study suggested that antidepressants could help calm it. *How many layers deep did these drug companies run?* I wondered. I was sort of offended by how quick everyone was to prescribe a mind-altering drug for every issue that came up. There had to be something else going on here, another answer. I decided that I would revisit my chronic itch issue after I returned from Chicago. Christmas was around the corner and, once again, I was going back home to see my family. Although I had hoped Oliver would come with me, he opted to go to Brazil with Josh and a couple of other clients.

Oliver was really impressed with how cool I had been with this plan. He told me the girlfriends of the other guys he was traveling with went ballistic when they were informed their boyfriends were spending the holiday without them, while I had been "unexpectedly" supportive. Little did he know that I saw this trip as the final chapter in his bachelorhood. In my mind's eye, there were reasons to believe this: Oliver had just bought a house I told him to buy, he was asking me for decorating input, and…we were spending the week after Christmas together. I was happy to fly back to Chicago solo and have some down time.

In my family, we take turns opening our Christmas gifts while gathered in a circle around the tree; that way, everyone can comment on what each person received, and Christmas isn't over in four seconds flat. My mom is always the one to pass out the presents, and she always saves the most profound gift for last.

"Here you go, honey," she said, passing me a present wrapped in green and red tissue.

I shook the box for effect, but I didn't hear any movement or rattling inside. *Definitely not jewelry*, I thought, as I tore off the wrapping and took in the title of the book confronting me.

"*He's Just Not That into You?*" I asked, confused.

Everyone got quiet, except my sister. "Hey! You gave that book to the wrong daughter," she said. "I'm the single one who needs a boyfriend."

"No…. I gave it to the right daughter," my mom insisted, before running into her bedroom and locking the door behind her. She never had been comfortable with rocking the boat or conflict. Which is why it was so frickin' ironic that she just got so good at rocking mine. An awkward silence loomed over the room.

Then the epiphany:

"Maybe my itch is from Oliver not being that into me," I hypothesized to no one in particular.

My sister looked down to avoid eye contact. I quickly hopped up off the couch and screamed "Thanks, mom!" before running downstairs to my bedroom, where I spent the next two hours reading the book from front to back. Then I called Oliver in Brazil.

"I think we should break up." I blurted before he could even say "hello."

"Why?" he replied in confusion.

"Because you're just not that into me," I declared.

"How so?" he asked, oddly gleeful.

Oliver always loved a good debate, especially one that involved my criticisms of him. In fact, as he begged me to read him sections from a book that described everything he'd done wrong, it occurred to me that Oliver had always been more interested in my criticisms of him than in my compliments to him. After I read an hour of excerpts that nailed Oliver to a tee, we both just laughed.

"Seriously, what couples do this?" I asked.

"Amy, I love you with every bone in my body," he said.

"Not according to this book."

"Look, it's just a book," he said. "I don't want to break up with you."

Because I had just given him every opportunity to get out of our relationship and he didn't jump at it, I thought maybe the book was wrong and tested him with the ultimate milestone.

"Then we should have no problem being engaged by my birthday in April," I said, before hanging up and hopping into another oatmeal bath. I was desperate to get out of my skin and resolve my new self-diagnosis.

When I got back to Los Angeles, I bumped into Chloe at the mailboxes in our courtyard. Chloe knew all the best healers in town. Massage therapist. Shaman warrior. Colonic master. Chinese herbalist. You name it, and Chloe could connect you to your next guru. She asked me how Oliver and I were doing. I told her we were great. "Then why does it seem like you're about to blow?" she replied.

I knew Chloe just wanted the best for me. But her astuteness sometimes was annoying because you could never hide from her. She was also one of those friends you hate to love so much because she's so unfairly gorgeous. She was a cross between Sienna Miller and Molly Simms. She had long blonde hair with the perfect amount of natural curl, an infectious smile that brought men to their knees, and a right eye that winked automatically (at both women and men) the minute she said hello. In a nutshell, Chloe was every woman's worst nightmare because she was bewitching in a way you were not. I was obsessed with this new glow she was sporting that made her look all of fifteen years old, and after she was so blunt with me, I was blunt with her. "Okay. What's going on?" I asked as we sifted through our junk mail in the courtyard. "You look like a teenager."

She told me she was seeing a cranial therapist in Santa Monica named Dr. Armstrong. She said it fell under the umbrella of a chiropractor, but instead of giving adjustments to your bones, he made adjustments to your energy. She said he was a healer who had the ability to unlock all of the doors inside of you, helping you to release your stuck chi. Apparently, just yesterday, she'd had some extraordinary emotional release after he held his hand above her knee cap, which had caused her to scream uncontrollably while lying on his table. Although I was skeptical, I wasn't the one sporting the dewy glow. Perhaps Dr. Armstrong could help me with my itch? I asked Chloe for his number. She said to make sure to tell his office that she referred me to him. "Otherwise, you could wait upwards of a year," she winked.

"I'm sure," I said, winking back. I called Dr. Armstrong's office to make an appointment the following morning, and his receptionist told me his next availability was in six months. I mentioned that Chloe had referred me.

"How's tomorrow at 2:00 p.m.?" she asked.

"Awesome," I said, winking through the line.

When I arrived at Dr. Armstrong's office, I was asked to fill out a form. The first question was, "Why are you here?" I thought about what I should write: *Anxiety? Spinster? Extravagantly seeking my own glow? Itching like mad? He can't commit?"* In the end, I only had the courage to jot down "itchy, can't sleep," before crossing it out altogether and not answering the question at all.

A few minutes later, a tall, slender man wearing Converse tennis shoes and green scrubs walked into the waiting room. He had short, cropped hair that was grey at his temples and perfect posture. He told me he was Dr. Armstrong. I followed him back to a sterile-looking examining room with a single bed and small window. He took the clipboard out of my hand and reviewed my questionnaire. "So, why are you here?" he asked, looking down at my scratched-out answer. Too embarrassed to discuss my crotch itch, I told him I wasn't sure. "Ah, a 'symptom minimizer,'" he said. "Go ahead and hop up onto the table. You can leave everything on but your shoes and lie face up."

Slipping off my ballet flats, I adjusted myself onto the table and closed my eyes. Dr. Armstrong went straight to my feet and began pulling on my big toes. "So, how's the wine intake?" he inquired. *How the hell does he know I drink wine?* I thought. Chloe was allergic to alcohol, so it wasn't like the "you are the company you keep" motto applied. I told him I drank a couple of glasses a night, as he moved on to my pelvis, where I prayed to God an exorcism was not about to take place. About forty minutes into my appointment, however, I was disappointed that, other than his ability to intuit that I drank wine, nothing had happened. Then I felt an excruciating pain in my heart. I thought Dr. Armstrong was pressing down on my chest. It pissed me off. Who did he think he was?

"Don't press so hard," I demanded.

"Amy, I'm not touching you," he replied.

I opened my eyes and looked down to see if he was telling me the truth. To my surprise, his hands, palms down, were about six inches above my heart center. I felt the tears percolating, but I didn't feel comfortable showing them to a doctor in Converse tennis shoes and kept them stuffed in my throat. I mean, what was really so bad in my life? I had parents who loved me, a job that paid my bills, a pretty apartment, and great friends. Society tells us we should be happy with my kind of life.

"It's okay," Dr. Armstrong said gently. "Let it go." But I just couldn't, not yet. I was ashamed that I could be in possession of a heart that hurt this much.

A few days before my thirty-sixth birthday, Oliver called, "Come over!" he said enthusiastically. I was surprised because Oliver was always off limits on

Sunday afternoons. It was his day to catch up on reading client scripts. When I got to his house, he opened the door and led me back to the kitchen. There were twenty votive candles lit on the counter. "Want a drink?' he asked, pulling out a chilled bottle of chardonnay.

OMG! Maybe he's going to propose! I felt a huge tingle in my stomach, but a couple of minutes later, he started talking about work.

"What is all this for?" I asked.

"I was just in the mood to light candles," he said, before asking me if I wanted to order a pizza. I was kind of pissed at how oblivious he was acting and told him I had made plans to have dinner with Chloe.

Then…

My birthday came. I had just left Oliver's house and was back at my apartment. It was around 10:00 in the morning, and the buzzer to my gate rang. I could only assume it was a delivery from my mother and picked up the phone.

Hello?"

"Come outside. I have something for you," Oliver said through the line.

Oliver never came over unexpectedly. It wasn't part of his DNA. Again, I felt my stomach flutter with delight. *Could it be?* Slamming down the phone, I dashed out of my apartment door to go let him into the courtyard. In all my excitement, I forgot that I could have buzzed him through the phone.

"Happy birthday!" Oliver said, holding out a dozen daisies I recognized from the wholesale flower market up the street. "Oh, and here's a massage certificate from Burke Williams Day Spa, too," he smiled nervously.

I suspected that the massage came from the stack of certificates that Oliver had already been gifted with by clients. I remembered seeing a pile of them stacked on top of his desk just yesterday. Everyone in Hollywood recycled gifts. I felt so stupid that I had even allowed myself to go to the place where there was a remote possibility of getting a ring. *Of course I wasn't getting a ring! I didn't go out and buy one for him to give to me.* On the verge of tears, I said goodbye to him, and he left for work.

Walking back into my apartment, I fetched a vase for my daisies because a vase is never included with one-step-up-from-a-weed flowers that you buy wholesale. My friend Chrissie peeked in after hearing all of the commotion. She had become one of my best friends and was a real fan of Oliver and me being together. I knew that she, more than anyone, had hoped to see a rock on my finger. So I felt especially humiliated in this moment and had to stay in denial for my own pride and dignity.

"Aren't they just gorgeous?" I said.

"They are," she said without making eye contact and dashed out. I knew what she was thinking because I was thinking the same thing. My thighs began itching like crazy. I picked up the phone and made an emergency appointment with Dr. Armstrong.

"Why doesn't he want to marry me?" I finally drummed up the courage to ask.

I was lying face-up on Dr. Armstrong's table, staring at the ceiling.

"You know, Amy, I'm an avid cyclist. Sometimes, I go into a bike store and see the thousand-dollar bike displayed in the center. Everything about it is great. The wheels. The spokes. The brakes. The frame. But for some reason, even though I can afford it, I respond to a different bike, one that isn't 'technically' as good. It just speaks to me more. It's like an energetic pull, an unspoken thing that attracts another," he said.

Over the next three weeks, I went to see Dr. Armstrong every Tuesday. With his help, I was finally starting to unearth some real feelings behind my itching skin. I was developing the consciousness to understand that the reason I had been prone to lower back pain and shallow breathing wasn't the result of being crazy, like I had always feared when I dated Richard, but the stress of not feeling rooted and secure in my world emotionally. More importantly, though, I realized that winning Oliver over was no way to live. Still... I wasn't ready to say goodbye and opted to spend the next three months itching.

In early July, I got a call from my commercial agent asking me if I could go on a last-minute audition for Budweiser in Santa Monica. I was clear across town and wearing an oversized sundress. I didn't look like a Budweiser girl; I looked like a Pilgrim. But I didn't have time to go home if I had to be there in an hour, so I told my agent I would go. It was the first call I'd gotten from him in months. But for the sporadic commercial audition, I wasn't going out on casting calls anymore.

When I arrived at the Bundy studios, the room was full of hundreds of gorgeous girls in tight jeans and tanks. I felt so frumpy. I thought about walking out but decided to sign in. I decided that I would wait fifteen minutes. If they didn't call my name by then, I would leave.

I took a seat on one of the long benches outside the four casting rooms. Two minutes later, a woman called my name. "That was fast," I said.

"All you have to do is slate your name and give us your profile," she said.

Five minutes later, I was in my car heading down Olympic in bumper-to-bumper traffic thinking, *what a waste of time.*

Later in the week, Oliver and I were driving down Sunset after having lunch at the Standard Hotel and my phone rang. It was my agent telling me I booked the commercial and that it was shooting next week.

"I don't even have to go on a callback?' I asked.

"Nope! They said you were perfect!"

I hung up the phone all smiles. "I booked Budweiser."

"Oh my God! No way. That's great. Congratulations," Oliver said.

He seemed really excited and proud of me. Although I couldn't prove it, deep down, I felt the reason he was so enthusiastic about this booking was that Budweiser made kind of a statement: a Bud girl was thought of as a model type of girl, like the one we saw in San Francisco who Oliver said was just the type his agency would love to represent.

When I arrived on the Budweiser set a few days later, there were two other girls in wardrobe with me. One looked like a Victoria's Secret model and the other looked like an Amish woman. I asked them if they were part of the crew. They told me they were talent, and that they had booked the commercial, too. An hour later, we were called onto the set for a rehearsal. The director came up and introduced himself. Then he lined us up like bridesmaids about to walk down the aisle. He put the Amish girl first, then me, then the Victoria's Secret girl. He told us he was going to roll tape and that he would gesture when he wanted each of us to walk into the mock bar they had set up in the studio. *Easy enough*, I thought.

A few moments later, the director screamed "action" and they rolled this song: "From the moment you walked through the front door, I knew one thing to be true. You were the prettiest girl I ever did see (go Amish Girl), until this other girl walked in after you (go Amy)."

Wait! I was the second prettiest girl? Suddenly clear on why I booked Budweiser, I felt so humiliated as I strolled into frame and wondered how the Amish girl they had pegged as the third prettiest must have felt. In this moment, I was done with acting for good. When I told Oliver about what had happened, I could see his wheels churning, like he didn't want to settle for the second prettiest girl. And I knew Oliver and I were done, too. It was time to let him go into the bike shop and pick out the ten-speed he wanted. Clearly, it wasn't me.

That Sunday, before I left Oliver's house to go to a matinee alone, we agreed to meet up for dinner at 7:00 p.m. But on my way to the matinee, I started crying so hard I couldn't stop and had to pull over. My tears were the size of grapes. I hadn't cried like this since being off antidepressants. But now, here I was. No more Band-Aids. No more denial. Just me— on the side of the road. My phone rang at 6:59 p.m. on the nose. I knew Oliver knew he was walking on thin ice. His calls usually came twenty minutes after when he promised he would call, something I always blamed on the absent-minded professor thing. *But not tonight*, I thought. Tonight, he was more than capable of remembering the time. He knew how to do it.

"I'm on my way over to pick you up," he said cheerfully.

"I don't want to go to dinner at 7:00," I replied.

"Then how about 7:30?' he barked back.

"No…what I mean is, I don't want to go to dinner with you at 7:00 or ever."

There was a dead silence for several seconds. I could hear Oliver thinking.

"Why not?" he asked.

"Because we're breaking up, Oliver."

"But I don't want you to break up with me!" he said firmly. "I love you with every bone in my body."

"Please, Oliver. I have to go."
Click.

"It looks like you've lost a lot of weight," Dr. Armstrong said, as I hopped off his table and pulled up my pants because they fell down my waist. I told him I had no idea how. Although it had been over a month since Oliver and I broke up, I hadn't been dieting.

"I can't tell you how many women this happens to after they come to see me," he said. Then he told me that weight is a form of protection, and that when you let go of the emotional garbage being stored in the body, oftentimes the weight just falls off all by itself. It made sense. I was amazed by how much lighter I was feeling from the work we had done together.

"Guess my baggage finally fits in the overhead compartment," I said.

He gave me a cautionary look. I didn't realize, like he did, that I still had another suitcase I needed to dump.

CHAKRA FOUR & FIVE

Jake and Me
September 2006—December 2006

"A spiritual warrior is conscious of each
action, but not necessarily aware of the entire
purpose of a particular mission. A spiritual
warrior knows to serve the true King, to act in
relation to the higher consciousness, but has
not necessarily awakened the upper chakras
of the heart and the brow and the intuition."
—Carolyn Myss

Five months after breaking up with Oliver, I was getting ready to head back to Chicago for Christmas. I opened my closet and reached for the large plastic storage bin that contained all my winter sweaters. A lot of random stuff was piled up on the shelf, and a stack of greeting cards from my mom fell out in front of me.

> *2004: "Amy, I know this is going to be the year that you will meet the man of your dreams. I just know it, darling."*

> *2005: "Darling Amy, he didn't deserve you, but I know he's around the corner."*

> *2006: "Daughter, I know this is going to be a year of falling in love. Just trust."*

I felt sick and walked across the hall to see if Chrissie would join me on the patio for a drink. She was packing for another Christmas vacation in Aspen with her longtime, soon-to-be-hubby boyfriend, Ben, stuffing each and every gorgeous item of clothing she owned into her suitcase. "There's no brass ring in packing light!" she said, pulling a few more items from her closet.

A few minutes later, Chrissie and I were sipping chardonnay on the patio. As we looked over our romantic courtyard, I told her how much I wished I were going away for Christmas with someone special. I was choking back tears.

"Why don't you come to Aspen with us?" she asked. "Ben's brother's room has two double beds, and he won't even try to sleep with you."

"Gee thanks," I replied.

"You know what I mean," she said.

"I know," I replied. "I guess it would just remind me of Oliver," I continued, choking back tears.

Topping off my glass with a little more wine, Chrissie gasped.

"You know what?" she said. "I just thought of someone really awesome I should set you up with." She said that he was a friend of Ben's brother and that his name was Jake. She told me he was married once before but came from a nice family and really wanted to get married again and have kids. He was from Chicago like me and lived in New York.

"New York?" I asked dubiously.

She told me not to worry, that he came to L.A. all the time.

"And best of all," she added, "I just remembered he's going to be in Chicago over Christmas. You guys should meet up for a coffee."

Silence.

"You are going back home again for Christmas, right?" she asked.

"Would you expect anything less?"

I told her to give Jake my number.

On the recommendation of a high school friend who still lived in Chicago, I told Jake to meet me at Ethel's. Apparently, it was the new hot spot in Lincoln Park for coffee or "if things are going 'really well' a chocolate martini," my friend said. The next day, I was horrified to see a man with a football player's frame standing in front of a pink gingerbread house. Ethel's looked more like a place to read fairy tales to three-year-olds than a sexy day-date spot. Quickly introducing myself, I apologized for the ambiance and stepped inside, where I tripped over several pink and white helium balloons that littered the floor. Jake immediately put me at ease by saying how great the coffee selection was as I scanned the board for a chocolate martini to no avail.

We found a table upstairs where, miraculously, there were no screaming kids. In my new pink Uggs and puffy white North Face jacket, I felt a little too Dallas-Cowboy-cheerleader-meets-Michelin-man. Worse, I matched the color scheme of Ethel's Coffee House. Not that I had a choice. It was freezing outside, and the jacket and Uggs were early Christmas gifts from my mom because I forgot my jacket and socks back in L.A. Sliding off my coat so Jake wouldn't think I was as fat as my down jacket made me look, I immediately felt his eyes graze across my chest in search of breasts. Thankfully, I'd always loved my "B" cup. I asked him how he knew Chrissie. "I don't," he said.

God love Chrissie.

Jake had beautiful blue eyes and a head full of thick, chestnut brown hair. He definitely would never have to worry about going bald. For the next hour, we discussed friends and work and family. Although he was built like a football player, I learned he was an English major at an Ivy League. Then, without thinking, because I'd grown comfortable, I mentioned that Chrissie had told me he'd been married. "Well, technically, I still am," he said.

God help Chrissie and where is that chocolate martini when you need one?

"But she's dating other women back in New York, so I won't be for much longer."

Jake shifted uncomfortably in his chair as he confided in me about his ex, Andrea, and how divorce was imminent. I could see the vulnerability behind his magnificent blue eyes and put my hand on his.

"You will be okay," I said, sharing a moment of eye contact that felt a little too intimate for two people who just met at Ethel's. Shifting my body uncomfortably, I accidentally kicked his foot (hard) underneath the table with my pink Ugg.

"Ouch!" he screeched.

"Sorry!"

"I'll never wash off the pink," he said, looking at my cheesy colored boots.

"Then I'm not sorry," I flirted back.

Jake asked me if I ever made it to New York. I told him rarely and asked him how often he came to Los Angeles. "Next to never," he said.

God forgive Chrissie.

Outside of Ethel's, Jake asked me what the best way to connect was. I told him we weren't exactly neighbors. "I have a lot of frequent flyer miles," he said.

I offered him my email verbally, hoping he'd reach out again. "If you're smart enough to remember it, perhaps we'll stay in touch," I said.

Six weeks after meeting Jake, Chrissie called and invited me to her thirtieth birthday celebration in New York. Although she kept her apartment across the hall from me, she was spending most of her time back East with Ben. I missed her desperately, and told her I would love to come out. The dinner would be hosted in the wine cellar of some amazing restaurant in the Village. I asked her if she would invite Jake. I hadn't heard from him since the day we met at Ethel's but figured *why not?*

Arriving the afternoon of Chrissie's birthday, I went to the restuarant early to help her light candles and organize the seating arrangements. The setting was super romantic, reminding me of Tuscany. I put Jake's place setting on my left because I'm a lefty and knew this meant we'd bump elbows all night. Then I dashed upstairs to find a bathroom. I wanted to apply some lipstick before everyone came. When I reached the top step, I bumped smack into Jake. He was the first guest to arrive.

"You never responded to my email," he said reproachfully.

"You sent one?"

"Quite a long one, the day after we met."

"I never got it," I replied, fantasizing about what our first kiss would be like, before darting past him to go gloss my lips for his.

Prior to the sit-down dinner, guests mingled around the table, sipping on prosecco. Jake was across the room, talking to Ben's brother while I chatted up some guy. I could feel Jake looking over and raised my gaze to meet his. Just like at Ethel's, the moment our eyes met, there was an intimacy that suggested we'd known each other much longer than we had. I nodded my head for him to come over, and for the rest of the party, he never left my side.

After closing down the restaurant, a group of us piled into a cab and went to a local hot spot called the Soho House. Somewhere between getting out of the cab Jake and I shared with four other people and the elevator ride we took up to the Soho House with these same people, we got so lost in each other's eyes that we forgot to get off the elevator. We found ourselves standing in a vacant room on another floor. Jake leaned into me until our mouths touched and gave me a kiss that stopped time. I once heard that the first kiss is a pretty good indicator of what is to follow; this must be true because the following morning I awoke to the biggest blizzard New York City had seen since 1941, grounding all airplanes. Time had stopped. I was officially, indefinitely, stuck in New York.

Seeking out a pair of boots from Chrissie's closet, I hoped Jake would call. I had their entire Chelsea loft to myself. Ben had told me the night before he was surprising Chrissie with a weekend getaway for her birthday. I trudged through several blocks of fluffy, knee-deep snow in search of a coffee shop, the streets full of kids engaged in team snowball fights and cross-country skiers shooting past high-rise buildings. Finally, I came across a local French bistro. Noticing Ethan Hawke at a corner table, I stepped inside when my phone rang.

"Where are you?" Jake panted through the line. "I'm running in your neighborhood."

I grabbed a menu to find my exact whereabouts. "Le Gammine," I said, pulling the name and address of the café off the menu.

Not five minutes later, Jake walked through the door. He obviously had been running towards Chrissie and Ben's Chelsea loft in pursuit of me. His thighs looked strong through his black nylon running pants, which the melting snow had rendered see-through. He leaned across the table and gave me a peck on the cheek. "Let's get out of here," he said. It was all I could do not to jump him right then and there.

On the way back to Ben and Chrissie's loft, Jake stopped into a corner market and picked up a fire log and a bottle of wine. I could feel his eyes grazing my behind and asked him what he thought. "Good," he laughed, giving it a pat. The rest of the afternoon Jake and I lounged in front of a fire, sipping char-donnay and kissing. But we talked, too. I found out his dad was a real estate tycoon and that he had two brothers who lived back in the Midwest. He liked the autonomy of New York because his family was so active in Chicago. He told me he'd been separated for three years. It seemed like an unusually long time to finalize a divorce, especially since they didn't have children. Maybe it was complicated because of the family situation. I gathered from our conversation that his family was sort of a big deal. At least he was being open about it. It showed he had nothing to hide. As the final embers dimmed, I told Jake it was time to go. As he pleaded for a few more kisses, I walked him to the door. "You are incredible," he said as the elevator doors closed behind him.

The following morning, I made a trek to Zara's to buy a warmer coat. It was still snowing, so I wanted to stroll through Central Park. On my way there, Jake called and asked if he could join. He said he'd just wrapped up a meeting not far from me. I still wasn't clear what he did for work. All I knew was, just like yesterday, he seemed to be able to get to my exact whereabouts within three minutes. Strolling hand in hand through Central Park, I felt more comfortable than I ever had with a man. *Was this really happening?* I honestly felt like I was falling in love with someone I'd spent less than twenty-four hours with. It felt ridiculously wonderful.

From the looks of his two-bedroom apartment in the West Village, I would never have suspected that Jake came from some important family. There was dog hair on the carpet; his couch sagged in the middle; and the arms on his club chair were soiled with cabernet stains.

"Looks like you enjoy your wine more than me," I remarked, chuckling. He opened the windows for some fresh air and told me the cleaning lady was coming the next day. I felt bad. It wasn't my intention to embarrass him. I would have liked Jake if he lived in a storage locker and came from two apes. Changing the subject, I asked him where his dog was. He told me that Daisy was with his mama for the week because he had recently been out of town. I assumed mama was the owner of the kennel Jake kept her at when he traveled.

Somewhere in between eating take-out and kissing, Jake grabbed his laptop off the dining room table and read me the email he sent after our blind date at Ethel's. It was almost a page long, confessing what a great connection he thought we had and mentioning that he hoped we would see each other again soon. All that time, I'd figured he just gave me the blow off. But now he was telling me that he was so disappointed that I hadn't responded. Going into my email account, I showed him that I really had never received it. "I guess Hotmail and AOL aren't compatible," he said. Then we talked and kissed, and talked and kissed, and talked and kissed some more.

Two hours into swapping saliva, I was nauseated and got up to use the bathroom. On the way there, I accidentally opened the door to what looked like a second bedroom. It was hard to tell because I couldn't see anything through the clothes piled up to the ceiling in every corner of the room. Jake immediately redirected me to the bathroom door directly across the hall. He seemed embarrassed by the mess. "I use this room as my walk-in closet," he told me.

A couple minutes later, the airlines called and told me they could get me out on an early morning flight the next day. The reality that my afternoons with Jake would be coming to an end made my heart sink, but it was time to go home. I told them I'd take the last seat. When I hung up, Jake had a sad look on his face. He joked that it was time to program all my information into his phone. Even though he'd been calling me all week, I guess he still hadn't officially added me to his contacts. So I gave him my home number, my address, and my office email. After he finished inputting all my information, a smile that was hard to pinpoint spread across his face. Sadness? Guilt? Relief?

"What is it?" I asked.

"You're now the first person...woman... to show up on my phone in over six years. It was always Andrea," he said nostalgically.

It took me a couple of seconds to catch on. Then I realized what he meant: "m" comes before "n": _**Am**_y. _**An**_drea.

"Are you good with that?" I asked gently.

"Yeah," he replied. "I love it."

When I landed back in Los Angeles, there was an email from Jake waiting in my inbox. "You are treacherous to my focus," it read.

Then, the following morning, a text came over my phone. "Can I come see you this weekend?"

I nearly fell off my chair with excitement and ran across the hall to tell Chrissie, who had just gotten back the day before. "He didn't offer to stay at a hotel?" she asked. I told her that didn't even come up. "Well, I think it's presumptuous that he didn't offer," she said. *Who cares what Chrissie thinks?* I thought. *The man of my dreams is coming out to see me.* Clearly, it had paid off not to sleep with him in New York.

The day of Jake's arrival, I wanted everything to be perfect. Before I left for the airport, Chrissie stopped by and gave my place a once over. I'd bought flowers, stocked the fridge, and had a little care package for him perched on my counter.

"Put a stack of books on your nightstands and dresser," Chrissie said. "Men find women who read a lot more interesting."

For a girl who didn't care what her friend thought, I immediately did as I was told. I thought it was a good suggestion. I was a big reader and had lots and lots of books stacked in piles underneath my bed. Why not put them on display? It's not like it was false advertising.

When I pulled up to the terminal, a huge grin spread across Jake's face when he saw me through the windshield. He looked gorgeous in his jeans and sweater. The minute he hopped in my car, we locked lips until a cop pounded on my window, waving a ticket book. Then we got stuck at our first stoplight. "Red light," Jake whispered in my ear, as he leaned over and kissed me. He continued this at every light we got stopped at on La Cienega Boulevard until it became a little game where I would follow up with "green light" all the way back to my place.

After we walked into my apartment, I wasn't sure if I should rip off Jake's clothes or offer him some of the rotisserie chicken I'd picked up for dinner. Luckily, I decided to pull the bird out of the oven. He gobbled the whole thing down. Then I gave him the gift bag I'd made up with various sunscreens and a note that read: "Welcome to the California sunshine."

"Thanks for making me feel so welcome," he said, pulling me towards him.

Then....

The clothes went flying off, and all I can say is..."Matt *who*?"

The following morning, I left Jake in bed to make breakfast. When I returned with a tray of fresh fruit and scrambled eggs, he was perusing through my stack of novels. "I love all your books everywhere," he said.

God love Chrissie.

Jake pulled me onto the bed, and we snuggled next to each other in comfortable silence for several minutes. "I keep fantasizing about you pregnant in a sundress and flip-flops," he said. All my married guy friends told me things could happen fast when a man believed you were the one. Their exact words were "When you know, you know."

As the sun shone through my bedroom window, I suggested we head to the beach. Jake thought that sounded wonderful, so we took a scenic drive down Sunset Boulevard until we arrived at the boardwalk.

A woman rollerbladed by with a golden retriever that looked exactly like Jake's dog.

"I forgot to ask you where you board Daisy when you travel," I said.

He looked at me in confusion. "Andrea always takes the dog," he replied. "We share her."

So that's the mama. I thought it was odd that they still had joint custody of Daisy after being separated for three years. But it was too soon to share this opinion, so I just made a mental note that they could share a dog and I could bear his children. But it bothered me all day.

Later that night, when Jake was in the shower, I called Polly. She was a huge dog lover and volunteered for all the local dog rescue places around town. I asked her what she thought. Polly assured me that dogs are like kids for some people and no good parent would walk away from their kid. She told me I had to relax on this one.

Two weeks later, I was back at JFK. When I walked out of the terminal, Jake was leaning against his car, holding flowers—Daisy was at his side, wagging his tail—and my last-row-coach-backache (which was the only ticket I could afford) was forgotten. No one greets people at the airport in New York, let alone brings their dog. A couple of cold beers on ice, along with a bottle of water, were waiting for me on the passenger seat. Daisy hopped right onto my lap and licked my face as I got into the car. "Wow, someone likes you,"

Jake said approvingly. "She never does this." We were off to a good start, I thought, covered in slobber.

When we got back to Jake's apartment, I was truly tickled as he copied everything I did. There was a rotisserie chicken in the oven; the sheets and floors had been scrubbed; and the same flowers that had been at my house were on the table. Putting my purse down on the counter, I noticed a card perched up against a glass. It was from Andrea: "Your eyes have never looked more clear. You seem so happy." *Why was Andrea still looking into his eyes?* Without mentioning a word, I immediately threw my arms around Jake to claim him. He was mine.

The following day, Jake and I strolled through the Village. Daisy was with us, which was somewhat annoying because we had to stop every other block and coax her to keep walking. Plus, I wanted all of Jake's attention and Daisy was getting most of it. I offered Daisy a cookie I'd bought and watched her gobble the whole thing down. "Do you want to walk her?" Jake asked. Seeing an opportunity to bond even more, I told him I'd love to. The second Jake passed the leash, Daisy sat on her butt and wouldn't budge. I tried coaxing her with another treat, petting her tummy, and nudging her by the collar, to no avail. Jake took back the leash and began petting her ears ferociously.

"Do you miss your mama?' he asked.

Daisy howled. Jake laughed. I cringed.

Later that night, we met up with Chrissie and Ben for sushi. Ben and Jake's families were friends, so they went way back. Ben asked me how my flight in was. I told him Jake had a cold bottle of beer waiting for me at the airport. "Ah…so you picked her up at the airport?" he said, winking at me in approval. Clearly, Ben was looking out for me, and Jake had just passed a big test in his book. It was just what I needed to feel secure after the whole dog incident earlier that day.

Then the following day, Jake asked me if I would go look at a few apartments with him. He said he was thinking about buying a place and really wanted my input. I was delighted. Hopping into a cab, we headed across town to see an apartment that overlooked the Hudson River and had a ton of natural light. As we stood in the living room, checking out the views with the Realtor, Jake turned to me.

"Could you live here?"

It was the question I had always hoped Oliver would ask.

Over the next several months, Jake and I took turns getting on planes to see each other every two weeks. We never fought, took long jogs along the Hudson, and the sex was extraordinary. Come June, Jake invited me to his parents' lake house outside of Chicago. Apparently, it was some notable home, and his mom was throwing it a hundred-year-anniversary party. I'd never been to an anniversary party for a house before and spent two weeks putting together perfect outfits to impress her.

The party was a catered dinner hosted underneath a tent fit for a royal wedding. During dinner, his parents stood up on behalf of the whole family and thanked everyone for coming. After acknowledging their three sons, Jake's mom made a special introduction of me. I was about to fall over in my chair. I think Jake was equally surprised because his jaw dropped. By night's end, over twenty guests walked up and introduced themselves to me. *So this is what it would have felt like to be famous*, I thought to myself. When everyone was gone, Jake and I embraced for a slow dance underneath the tent as Jake's mom watched from a distance. "My parents love you," he said.

The following morning, I was in the kitchen getting a coffee. Jake's mom walked up.

"I have good tips on a fast engagement," she winked. It seemed I had won her over. Saying goodbye to Jake at the airport that Sunday was the hardest it had ever been. I didn't want to have to keep saying goodbye anymore. It was exhausting, emotionally and physically.

Two weeks later, I was back in New York. While strolling Daisy through the Village that Saturday, I commented on this cool walkup building we passed that was under construction, a few blocks from Jake's house. "I just made an offer on the top floor," Jake told me.

I immediately dropped his hand. Hurt and flabbergasted, I told him I'd love to see it. He said there wasn't anything to see. When I mentioned architectural renderings, he was elusive. How did we go from "Could you live here?" to this? My instincts told me that someone from the anniversary party at his parents' lake house mentioned to Andrea that his family had introduced me publicly. Threatened that we may be getting serious, she was playing him somehow. She wanted the comfort of knowing she would always own Jake's heart while having the freedom to explore the I-might-be-a-lesbian card.

Back at Jake's house, I was in the bathroom cleaning a soiled shirt and walked into the bedroom he "used as a closet" to get a hanger. I had not stepped foot in this room since the first tine I mistook it for the bathroom. When I opened the door this time, the room was spotless, allowing me to see everything I had failed to see before, like a dresser and a radiator, where a shrine of framed photographs of Andrea and Jake were perched. I had never seen Andrea before. She was really pretty. I bet I was her type.

Walking into the kitchen, I confronted Jake. He swore up and down that nothing was going on, that he was just the lazy guy who hadn't bothered to take down the pictures. I told him I had to go get some air and stormed out. Thirty minutes into my walk, Jake called and asked if he could join me. When we connected on the sidewalk, he had that sad I-love-you-but-I-don't–know-what-to do-with-you kind of look on his face, which is the worse kind, because I wanted him to know exactly what to do: dump Andrea and be with me.

"I feel like the weekend girl," I said. Without contradicting me, he took my hand in his, and we walked down the sidewalk in silence. In the distance, where the twin towers once stood, was a gaping hole in the New York skyline. A sorrow I hadn't felt in a long time pulsed through me. I, too, felt like I might crumble.

Back in L.A., I felt really off center. Emotionally drained from the weekend and physically exhausted from all the plane rides, I remembered how much Kundalini had grounded me and decided to try another class. It had been so long that the yoga studio had moved. The new Golden Bridge was in Hollywood.

On the way there, a car swerved into my lane, forcing me to slam on my brakes and my horn. Usually, this wouldn't faze me, but that day it felt like a bomb had gone off in my ear. I immediately turned off the radio because the sound of the horn and music and brakes together was too much for my nervous system. I felt like Michael Douglas right before he went postal in the movie *Falling Down*.

The new studio was much bigger than the last one. It had a café, a bookstore, and a tea and wellness bar. A tranquil water fountain and lovely flower arrangements graced the entrance. Eastern rugs adorned the walls and soothing Sanskrit mantra was looping in the background. Yet the minute I walked through the front doors, I felt anything but relaxed and headed straight for the tea bar. With over twenty elixir combinations to choose from, I asked the twenty-something Brad Pitt look-alike working the counter what he'd recommend.

"Depends," he answered. "How long have you had emotional problems?"

I wanted to hurl my wallet at him but I would have missed, my hands were shaking so badly. Realizing I must have looked like a detoxing drug addict, I assured him all I was recovering from was another man and a near car accident on the way over. Then I huffed off, wishing him a dozen broken hearts by the time he was my age. It was so un-yogi of me.

Gurushabed, who owned the Golden Bridge with his wife Gurmukh, was teaching class that day. I rolled out my yoga mat in the front row, next to the wall. Gurushabad was already sitting cross-legged on stage, meditating. I sat down and closed my eyes, too. Before class began, Gurushadbad shared a story about a woman who'd recently approached him after one of his classes. She told him it was her first time doing Kundalini yoga and that she had really loved it. However, she said she wouldn't be back anytime soon because her habits weren't in sync with the yogic lifestyle. She smoked pot, drank alcohol, popped pills, and slept around. "Just add yoga," Gurushabed told her. "The rest will fall off without you having to do anything."

What a lovely story, I thought to myself. *Just add yoga.*

The following night, Chloe and I walked up to the Chateau Marmont for dinner. We were sitting on the star-studded patio, sipping chardonnay when I noticed Chloe shoot a flirtatious wink to Ben Stiller across the lawn. She'd had a few lines in his movie *Starsky and Hutch* and hoped he would remember her. Ten minutes later, he walked up.

"Your scene got a lot of laughs in the editing room," he said.

Chloe tilted her head just right and thanked him. Then he turned toward me.

"I'm Ben," he said, extending his hand.

"Yeah, I know all about your hundred-and-fifty-thousand-dollar pool," I said.

"Excuse me?"

Realizing I must have sounded like a crazy stalker, I told him I was Realtor and that I'd been to a dinner party several years ago with Matthew Perry at a house he once owned. The new owner had given me extensive details on the caissons required to support the pool he wanted to put in, should I ever have a buyer. Grasping that I wasn't going to show up in a ski mask, I saw Ben's shoulders relax.

"Well, you nailed the cost of the pool," he said, before telling Chloe once again that she had done a good job and walking away.

"I'm a little off after my trip to New York," I said to Chloe.

She looked me directly in the eyes and said I should consider signing up for teachers' training at Golden Bridge with her and Liz in a couple of weeks. "I just think it would be good for you," she said with concern.

Before I could reply, Amanda Peet walked up to say hello. She was having dinner with her fiancé,

Josh. They were getting married in New York in a few weeks and had invited Jake and me to their wedding. Ironically, Jake and Josh had gone to college together. The invitation was addressed to both of us and sent to Jake's place. As far as everyone knew, we were going strong because up until my last visit to New York, we were. Flashing me a concerned look, Amanda asked me if I was going to be okay seeing Oliver with his new girlfriend at the wedding.

"Of course" I was okay, I told her. "I'm super happy with Jake!"

"Glad to hear it," she said. "Don't fuck it up."

I wanted to scream, "Is there something on my forehead that says, 'I fuck up my relationships?'" But instead, I smiled the fakest smile I've ever drummed up.

"Roger that."

"Go back to the womb, the womb, the womb," a woman's voice whispered in a creepy tone.

I peeked over at Chloe and Liz who were sitting cross-legged next to me in a deep trance. *Really? I can't remember yesterday, let alone my mother's vagina.* Closing my eyes, I wondered how I ever got talked into coming to this three-hour rebirthing workshop.

"You are just a seed, a seed, a seed. In the womb, the womb, the womb."

Unbidden, the teacher's words brought back something Jake had said about how he pictured me pregnant in a sundress and flip-flops. *Dammit, Jake! Get out of my head. Breathe—in, out.* Phew. Better.

"There is light, light, light. In the womb, womb, womb."

Okay, this was getting weird: a womb with a view? What I needed was wine. I would pick up some chardonnay at Bristol Farms on my way home. Maybe a fire log, too.

"Visualize a little ball of white light going down a dark canal."

Instead, my mind wandered to a dark New York hallway, opening into a second bedroom, the former mess cleared away, photographs of Jake with Andrea everywhere.

"Inhale!"

The whole room erupted in breath. I looked over at Chloe, who was stretching her arms above her head, telling everyone how amazing she felt; Liz seemed equally excited. I, too, felt slightly better than when I walked in, despite not being able to focus, and began to roll up my mat.

"Have you decided if you are going to take teacher's training with us?" Liz asked, stretching her arm across her chest in my direction.

I told her I was pretty sure I'd failed womb reentry but I'd think about it, and I grabbed a registration packet from some Sikh girl wearing a five-foot turban on the way out.

Teachers' training was one weekend a month for eight months and followed a tight schedule. It went from 6:00 to 9:00 p.m. on Fridays and 9:00 a.m. to 6:00

p.m. on Saturdays and Sundays. I put down the packet and called Jake. We hadn't talked about anything but the weather all week, so I decided to open up and tell him I was thinking about getting certified. I said it was a big commitment that would keep me in L.A. for the next eight months. I hoped he'd argue, or at least show some reluctance, but he immediately perked up and said he thought I should go for it. Before this last trip to see him, I thought there was a real possibility I'd be moving to the East Coast. But he was a little too enthusiastic about my staying in LA for me to hold onto that fantasy anymore. He didn't want me. *Just say it and get it over with*, I thought, then pushed the thought out of my mind as quickly as it surfaced. The truth was, I couldn't take hearing it, not yet. It would mean going to the wedding to face Oliver and his new girlfriend alone. Amanda would look at me with pity. Another relationship fucked up. So, I pretended to believe he was being super supportive, before cutting the conversation short by telling him I was really tired and had to go to bed.

I woke the following morning in a puddle of drool on my couch after falling asleep to *When Harry Met Sally* for the fiftieth time. An empty bottle of wine on the coffee table reminded me why my head hurt. Shuffling to the bathroom, I downed two Advil. That would dull the hangover but do nothing for the hole in my heart. There were so many things I needed to change. I didn't know where to begin. Then, those three words came back to me: *Just Add Yoga*.

I called Golden Bridge to sign up for teacher's training that weekend.

"Four a.m.?" I objected. "The packet said we had to be here at 9:00!"

The same Sikh girl who'd given me the forms flashed me a smile. "Sadhana is optional," she assured me at that night's orientation.

Sadhana (pronounced *sod nuh*) is a daily spiritual practice, she explained. In Kundalini yoga, Sadhana starts before the sun is up and goes for two-and-a-half hours. Had I known about this part before giving them my non-refundable deposit a couple of days earlier, I might have reconsidered. When my alarm went off at 3:30 a.m., I was grumpier than a two-year-old being weaned off her binky. I was the girl who'd never been willing to get up this early to catch a flight to the tropics, and yet here I was getting up to chant with a bunch of Sikhs.

Without traffic, it only took Chloe and me four minutes down Sunset Boulevard to get to the yoga studio. I couldn't believe how many people were up at this time and hoped a cop wouldn't pull us over because, if one had, they would clearly think we were on drugs dressed alike in matching head-to-toe white, with lopsided head wraps (did I mention those?).

When we arrived, the yoga studio was so crowded we couldn't find a place to put our yoga mats. Stepping around, over, and on bodies in the dark, I finally managed to squeeze myself between two people already so deep in meditation they didn't notice me. A Sanskrit mantra called *Japji* was playing. Everyone was sitting in easy pose with their eyes closed and their hands in their laps. I didn't know any of the words to *Japji* but got into easy pose as a mouse skittered across my mat and disappeared. I was really afraid of mice and thought about moving, but I was so tired that I just closed my eyes and concentrated extra hard on the sound of the words. Before long, I fell into a state of deep relaxation. The next thing I knew, Gurushabed was telling us that yogi tea and granola were waiting for us in the café. Two-and-a-half hours had passed, and it felt like just five minutes. Although I'd hoped the meditation would distract me from thinking of Jake, I never suspected it would transport me through time and space. It was the most amazing thing I'd ever experienced, and I didn't want it to be over. I would never view Sadhana as optional again.

Of the twenty-five masters in the world certified to train Kundalini Yoga, four taught at Golden Bridge and were hosting my teachers' training. *Vanity Fair* magazine had just pegged Gurmukh, the owner and the most famous of the four instructors, as the Queen of Kundalini. She was the only person I knew who could take the simple Sikh wardrobe of a turban and *Kurta* and make it look runway ready. Her turban, neck, and wrists were always adorned with beautiful Indian jewel stones. She was a bit of a diva (in a good way), too.

Tej, on the other hand, was much more understated. She always wore a Timex style watch, white t-shirt, and flowing skirt. A mother hen, she took every hurting soul under her wing, especially if it was a good-looking guy.

Gurushabad led Sadhana. He was the mastermind running the studio and his wife Gurmukh's yoga schedule. Then there was Harijiwan, the teacher I knew nothing about, other than that he looked like John Lennon and encouraged Liz to take teacher's training.

Thank goodness the teacher's training weekends followed a tight schedule—less time to think of Jake. After Sadhana, a light breakfast was served. Then Gurmukh assigned us our first of three forty-day meditations. She said the reason for this timeframe was that it takes forty days to change a habit. If we missed a single day, even day thirty-nine, we had to start all over again. She told us to create an altar to do our meditations next to every day. A student asked her why. "Because altars, alter you," she said. "They are trigger points that redirect your psyche."

In all my years of going to Catholic Mass, I had never thought about the altar in this way. Yet every time I saw a cross hanging above the altar, or the chalice sitting on it, my mind was directed to the Last Supper. No matter what I'd been thinking about just moments before, both symbols changed the direction of my mind.

At the close of that first weekend, Harijiwan taught a workshop on *The Responsibilities of Being a Teacher.* He told us the reason that Kundalini yoga instructors wear all white is that white helps a teacher look divine and represents light. White is uplifting and represents all the seven colors (seven chakras).

Wearing a turban helps contain and balance the energy and is for the teacher's protection when handling the "powerful energies involved with teaching a Kundalini yoga class." The teacher trainers were encouraged to wear a head covering to protect them from headaches as well. It all made sense and took the weirdness I had attributed to the practice away.

Then, Harijiwan began chanting in a deep voice: "I am not a man, I am not a woman, I am not a person, I am not myself; I am a teacher," and it all seemed a little cuckoo again. *More cuckoo than Jake having pictures of Andrea up everywhere when he was claiming to be in love with me?* Angry with Jake for intruding into my thoughts again, I repeated these words with the rest of my classmates as Harijiwan instructed until we were dismissed.

The next morning, I was in dire need of two things: a hot bath for my sore muscles and a dress for Amanda's upcoming wedding in New York. It would be my first time seeing Oliver socially since our breakup, and my first time seeing Jake since the Andrea's-everywhere-in-your-apartment weekend. I was determined to look my best.

After soaking in the tub, I went to Neiman Marcus and charged three dresses on my credit card: a sophisticated, knee-length, black number that hugged my body at the butt; an electric blue sheath with a scooped back that accentuated my shoulder blades; and a light purple frock that made me look a little too pale and hit my thighs in all the wrong places, but had a nice Grecian vibe.

When I got home, I knocked on Chrissie's door and had her take a photo of me in each one, making sure to get side and back views. Ashamed of how self absorbed this all was, I emailed the photos to my mom, my dad, and my sister for their votes. Hands down, the black dress won. I returned the other two to Neiman's the following day. Then I headed to Frederic Fekkai to get a haircut. Explaining to the stylist how I wanted a little weight taken out of my shoulder-length bob and only the ends trimmed ever so slightly, she inspected my hair with her fingers and told me she knew exactly what to do. Then she spun me around in the chair to face her and started chipping into my hair. Twenty minutes later, she turned me back toward the mirror and smiled.

"Oh my God, what have you done?" I said.

My hair was up to my earlobes. It seemed in her book "a bob" with long layers meant a razor cut with straggly thin bits of hair left on the bottom to resemble the tail Mrs. Brady had on *The Brady Bunch*. I cupped my face in my hands and sobbed.

"I won't charge you for the haircut," she said, rushing off.

Everyone in the salon came over to help. One stylist named Yoshi thought hair extensions might work; another mentioned a wig shop on the corner. A third stylist had no suggestions at all because in the end: I had no hair left to do much of anything. I cried all the way home before barging into Chrissie's apartment, hoping that she would put me at ease because that's what friends do sometimes when you are hurting—lie to your face in order to make you feel better.

"Ugh!" she gasped. "What happened to your hair?"

That Thursday, I boarded the plane to New York feeling very insecure. About to be confronted with another wedding that wasn't mine, a boyfriend who wasn't who I thought he was, and an ex who didn't want to marry me, I tried to find comfort by twirling my long ponytail around my fingers, but I was met with a wispy strand of baby fuzz stuck against my bare neck instead.

"I am not a man, I am not a woman. I am not a person. I am not myself. I am a teacher," I repeated to myself as I took my seat in last row coach. *Why on earth did those words just pop out of my mouth?*

As we ascended above the smog-filled sky now blanketing Los Angeles, I ruminated on the teacher's oath that had made no sense to me just days earlier. I realized I'd spent so much of my life obsessing about my clothes, about the body I needed to have in order to fit into these designer clothes, and the perfect hair, that the essence of who I really was had gotten lost. Souls aren't defined by couture or color or shape. Souls expand beyond these boundaries. Souls are so much more. I took my own oath:

"I am not my haircut."

The days of Jake picking me up from the airport had ended months before. As I stood in the forty-five-minute cab line at JFK with frozen fingers, it occurred to me that I had no idea why, or maybe I did, but it was one of those things I hadn't been willing to see.

To my relief, Jake didn't notice the seven inches of hair missing from my head when I arrived at his place. He was too busy playing Atari with his college friend Tom who was also in town for the wedding and staying the night with us. After they finished their game, Tom asked me what I was wearing to the wedding. Delighted someone cared, I pulled my dress out of the garment bag and held it up to my chin.

"What about the shoes?" he asked.

I felt like Tom could be my new best friend and slid on my Lanvin heels, which I'd dyed black for the occasion.

"Those are gorgeous," he approved. "Just stunning!"

The ceremony was held at Amanda's alma mater, Friends Seminary, a Quaker school founded in 1786. The whole place was full of people I recognized from L.A. I took a seat with Jake in the second-to-last row pew because my backside was not my strong suit that night. The bra I wore was riding up at the back of my black dress, requiring a tuck-in every two minutes. And the low ponytail I managed to pull my hair back into was so short it resembled something you'd see on a pig's rear end. So of course, a few moments later, Oliver strolled in late with his girlfriend and took a seat in the last pew, directly behind me.

I am not my bra. I am not my haircut.

The bride and groom took their vows, but all my ears could focus on was the friction sound of Oliver's thigh being rubbed by his new girlfriend. Was she trying to start a fire on his suit's pant leg? Then I wondered which suit he was wearing. I knew them all by heart.

After the ceremony, I wanted to crawl under the pew. Instead, I turned around to face Oliver. He flashed me a big toothy smile, and we both said hello. It was my first chance to get a good look at the new girlfriend. With her toned arms and long brown hair, she looked just like Gabrielle Reece.

"Amy, this is Rachel," Oliver said proudly.

Smiling too big, I introduced them to Jake. Seeing Oliver with another woman was way more difficult than I'd thought it would be. I quickly excused myself to the bathroom to regroup. Amanda glided in behind me, looking like a bird about to take flight in her white-feathered gown.

"You look really good!" she said.

I thought it was very kind for the bride to pay me the compliment and quickly put the focus back on her. I told her I loved her dress, with its elegant spaghetti straps, black-sashed waist, and feathered bottom.

"Oscar de la Renta," she winked before heading back out.

Of course it was, I thought. All the Hollywood actresses get the big designers fighting to fit them.

A bus was taking the wedding guests to an undisclosed location for the reception in an effort to ditch any paparazzi. Jake and I were the last to board. As we took a seat toward the back, I realized I forgot my pashmina in the pew and told Jake. "How did you forget your pashmina?" he asked harshly. I wanted to scream, "How did you forget to get a divorce?" Not wanting to lose my cool and my wrap in the same evening, I ran off to retrieve it, leaving the bus to idle while everyone on it waited for me to return.

Jake and I were seated on the opposite side of the room from Oliver and his L.A. posse. As I looked around our table, I noticed something odd. Across from me sat the ex-girlfriend of the groom's agent. Next to me was Amanda's ex-best friend. I recognized her from a scene we were in together in *Whipped*. I remembered asking Amanda about her when we were neighbors and was surprised when Amanda said they'd lost touch.

"But you guys were so close," I'd said.

"Things change," Amanda shrugged.

Yes, they do, I thought. I was clearly at the reject table. Reaching for Jake's hand under the table, I asked him if he wanted to dance, but he told me he didn't dance. Then he excused himself and headed to the bar, where he spent the remainder of the night chatting with the bartender about football and drinking beer. Although it was a different set of players, I felt like I was reliving the nightmare of Sloan's wedding all over again.

By the end of the dinner, I was sitting all alone at the table. Oliver walked up and sat down next to me. I think he felt sorry for me. He asked me how my mom and step-dad were. He even asked if I was still spending time at my mom's beach house over the summer months. An overwhelming wave of emotion surged through me just being in his presence. I realized I might be no more over Oliver than Jake was over Andrea. But I was sure my feelings weren't reciprocated. So I just told him that his new girlfriend was pretty and that I was glad he seemed happy. Then I made my way back to the ladies' room to collect myself for the second time that evening. To my dismay, there was a line, and Oliver's girlfriend walked up behind me. She was checking me out, of course. When our eyes locked, all pretense dissolved, neither one of us said a word. The look on her face was as indecipherable as the *Mona Lisa* and left me with a chill.

After the reception, all the L.A. guests were standing outside trying to decide where to go next. "How about the Soho House?" Oliver suggested at random. I was transported back to the night Jake and I went there after Chrissie's birthday dinner. Getting lost in the memory of our first kiss, I looked over at Jake to see if he might be reminiscing about the same thing. But Jake didn't look like he was reminiscing about much of anything. After so much to drink, his head resembled that of a Raggedy Ann doll, rolling back and forth on his neck. *Of all nights*, I thought to myself.

Hailing a cab to take Jake home, I stared out the window and took in the city for what I sensed would be the last time in a long while. Being with the "almost" divorced guy had required the compassion and patience of a saint. Yet Jake had bestowed neither of these virtues on me tonight, even though he knew it was the first time I'd be seeing Oliver since our breakup. As I looked over at Jake slumped in the seat, I knew even if he hadn't gotten drunk and we had made it to the Soho House, it wouldn't have been the same. Jake had long since checked out of our relationship.

The next morning, as I was getting ready to head to the airport, a text came over my phone. To my astonishment, it was from Oliver and read, "You never looked more beautiful." For a split second I hoped maybe, just maybe. Then I remembered back to the afternoon he'd lit all those candles and summoned me over. I felt both full and empty. I had transcended my horrible haircut and left a good, loving impression on Oliver's heart. But I was alone again.

I don't know how I would have held it together as well as I did if not for the full schedule of teacher training classes at the Golden Bridge. Not wanting too much time alone with my thoughts of Jake and Oliver, I added an evening meditation class with Harijiwan. It was hosted in a small room off the main studio. Walking in this room for the first time, I felt like I'd stepped inside a genie's bottle. Floor cushions in different shades of orange were sprinkled all over the floor, glittery tapestries adorned the walls, and a huge gong was mounted in a stand next to Harijiwan.

As I rolled out my mat in the back, I noticed a pretty female student showing him a photo of some guy and asking him a lot of questions. After class, I asked her what it was all about. She told me he gave really good dating advice off of the face reading he did from photographs. Drumming up the courage to approach him outside, I poured out my whole sad story about how Jake couldn't divorce the lesbian.

"Is he sleeping with her?" he asked.

I told him of course not. She was a lesbian.

He looked directly into my eyes. His stare was so deliberate…a light bulb went off inside. *Of course he was sleeping with her. Andrea was a lipstick lesbian, aka the girl who thought it was fun to kiss a girl but who—in the end—decided she wasn't going to let Jake go. I wanted to cry, I was so depressed.* I asked Harijiwan how I could get both of them out of my head. I told him I felt so entangled in a love triangle, like a spider caught in its web. He told me to loop the healing mantra twenty-four hours a day in my house. He said it would help rebuild my nervous system and redirect my psyche, superseding all the negative chatter. Then, pretending to jot something down on his hand, he passed me a make-believe piece of paper.

"What's this?' I asked

"Your new prescription," he said. "One yoga class a day."

I told him it was a tall order considering I was also taking teacher's training.

"What else do you have going on?" he shrugged.

Absolutely nothing. Real estate was slow with an impending recession; the last audition I had was for cat litter; and I had no plane to catch, being newly single. I had some time to kill. Besides the eight teacher training weekends, we were required to take an additional twenty yoga classes to get certified.

That night, I downloaded the mantra on my iPod and pressed repeat. The first couple of nights, when I crawled into bed and listened to the words, all I did was cry. It was as if a million tears I had squashed down inside of me were coming out. It was not lost on me that Kundalini, which is represented by the serpent snake, means "to uncoil." I just didn't know there was so much sadness still residing in the nooks and crannies of me, and I hoped I would recoil soon.

Luckily, on Sunday, Gurmukh taught a class that left me feeling so giddy I might as well have been Julie Andrews. It also left me feeling so sore I couldn't walk for days because Gurmukh had students hold yoga postures forever. Then, there was a powerful morning class taught by Tej at 9:00 a.m. But she brought me so far out into the ether that after my third class with her I literally watched myself throw my wallet and car keys into the garbage can after finishing a salad in the café. Several minutes later, I realized what I had done and went to fish them out. I couldn't afford to be that spacey all day, even if flying that high felt sort of wonderful.

During my second weekend of teacher's training, I created a small altar on the bottom shelf of my bamboo nightstand and started my meditation every night before bed. The first few days, I didn't feel much of anything. Then on day four, halfway through the chanting, I felt this surge of energy, like restless leg syndrome of the genitals. I sprang out of cross-legged position and began to hop around like a jumping bean.

The next time I was at the yoga studio, Tej told me the sensation was old, stuck energy moving up out of my second chakra. I was surprised that the small act of chanting *SAA TAA NAA MAA* could have such a powerful effect and continued the meditation every night. Two weeks later, this sensation went away.

Then on day twenty, while staring at the tip of my nose, I felt an intense ache in between my brows. Again, I asked Tej about it. She said it was my third eye opening. "When you pray, you talk to God, but when you meditate, God talks to you," she said. Oh, how I hoped this was true. I was now thirty days into my meditation and nothing from God yet. But there was also less in my head about Jake, who was slowly receding from the top of my mind almost without my noticing. When I finally hit the forty-day mark, I felt especially agitated while silently chanting "Raa-Maa-Daa-Saa," Then—out of nowhere—I heard a voice direct me to:

"Go buy a filing cabinet, Amy."

"What?" I said, as I continued to sit crossed-legged and silently repeat the mantra.

"I said to go buy a filing cabinet," the voice repeated.

It wasn't exactly the exciting message from God I had anticipated.

The next day, I was in my kitchen, a sink full of dirty dishes, downing some orange juice when Chloe barged into my apartment without knocking and looked around.

"I think you need to get organized," she said. "I was up all night thinking about it."

"You mean like, I should buy a filing cabinet?"

"It just sort of came to me in my meditation," Chloe nodded, as she took one of my kitchen drawers out from its rollers, turned it upside down, and watched its contents fall onto my floor. "See… it's easy," she said, plopping herself down and proceeding to separate five years of random receipts into neat piles. "Who's this guy?' she asked, as she came across a photo, tucked inside some of the receipts.

"Oh, that's Sam," I said with nostalgia. "My boyfriend after college."

"You really do need to get organized," she said.

Almost as soon as I plopped myself down next to her to help, she said she had to go.

"How am I ever going to get through all of this alone?"

"*RA, MA, DA, SA,*" she said jokingly, before adding, "Look how far you've gotten already," and walking out the door, leaving me in a mountain of receipts.

Seven days later, every drawer had been excavated, and every receipt separated, shredded, or thrown out. Now the only thing left to do was clean off a chalkboard that was so cluttered with paper, I couldn't even see it anymore, let alone write on it. Except for a magnet, I swiped everything off with my hand, leaving just that one thing smack dab in the middle of the chalkboard: a square plaque with the single word FAITH.

One Tuesday night, while chanting in Harijiwan's meditation class, I noticed I was looking down at my own body. It felt like my soul had flown out of the top of my head and that life on the physical plane had been momentarily suspended because there I was, looking down at Amy below. Seeing myself down on the earth realm meditating made me think the other side wasn't too bad; it was kind of peaceful floating above all the bullshit, actually. Then Harijiwan struck the gong, and, just like that, I was back inside myself again. I felt this little sense of peace wash over me. In that moment, I knew I would be fine on the other plane, too. It was as if any fear of the unknown had just melted away.

When class was over, Harijiwan asked me how I was.

"Happy," I said decisively.

A satisfied smile spread across his face. I realized it was the first time I'd ever responded to the question this way. Usually, it was, "Good, but…" or "I'm fine, I guess." But today, I felt organically happy. I realized it wasn't due to some outside circumstance, like a new boyfriend or a real estate deal or an acting gig. It was just something that came from deep inside me for no reason in particular.

So…

I was surprised that come the next month's teacher's training weekend, the other thing consuming me was extreme jealousy toward Chloe, who looked especially gorgeous and dewy that Saturday. All the guys loved her, and not one guy had looked at me in months. I couldn't even look at her when I walked into that afternoon's workshop and sat on the opposite side of the room, even though she had saved me a spot next to her.

A guy named Gurudhan was teaching the session. He told us we were going to do a special exercise and gave everyone a blank sheet of paper, a pencil, and some tape. He instructed us to attach the blank piece of paper to our backs with the tape and walk around the room. Then he said to stop when we passed a student we knew to write the one word that came to mind and best described how we viewed this person. Of course, you couldn't see what anyone had written on your own back, only what had been written on the backs of the people you stopped. By the time I passed Chloe, her back displayed the words "sexy," "mysterious," "gorgeous," and "shockingly beautiful." I put on my best fake smile and wrote down the word "gorgeous" on her back. Then I pursed my lips and batted my eyes to everyone who stopped me so I might get some of the same words Chloe had.

"Okay," Gurudhan said. "Please wrap up whatever you are writing and then sit down quietly to review your piece of paper by yourself."

As nonchalantly as possible, I pulled the paper off my back and slithered down the wall to read my words: "charming," "funny," "bubbly," and "nice." *What the hell?* Why didn't I get at least one "sexy" or "mysterious"? "Nice" is the word I use to describe all the guys I'm not interested in. And who cares about "funny" or "bubbly"? I am not *bubbly.* I am *deep.* At this point, I don't think I was hiding how bummed out I must have been because Chloe approached.

"I didn't get a chance to write anything on your back," she said.

I gave her my piece of paper and rolled my eyes behind her back.

"Here you go, darling," she winked, before fluttering off to the bathroom like a magical fairy with gold dust around her.

I looked down at what she wrote about me, which only agitated me more because I didn't believe her.

"A gorgeous beauty that's brighter than the stars."

I didn't even look at guys anymore. I noticed that they didn't look at me, either. So that Friday, when Annie invited me to join her for a drink in Echo Park, I thought maybe it was time to get out of my yoga clothes. Annie was very "Echo Park." She was drawn to areas as they were gentrifying. Before moving to L.A., she lived in an area of San Francisco called the

Mission. Gunshots could be heard going off there every night, but new restaurants with rave reviews were popping up there, too.

The minute I walked into the bar, I felt out of place. The house music was too loud, the bar too crowded, and everyone was draped in black. For the past four months, I'd lived in white clothes and only listened to Sanskrit mantra. Annie ordered a glass of wine at the bar; I ordered a club soda with a splash of cranberry. I had always been her wine buddy, but now I practically lived at Golden Bridge and wasn't craving alcohol like I used to.

After we got our drinks, we found a corner table. Annie saw a gal she knew and told me she'd be right back. I nodded as a man tapped me on the shoulder.

"Mind if I take a seat for a minute?" he asked.

I told him to go ahead.

He was tall and lean and had dark hair. Handsome—if you were out looking. But all I wanted to do was go home and take a bath and do my meditation. He proceeded to introduce himself and ask my name.

"Let me buy you a drink?" he said. I told him I was good and scanned the room for Annie. Another loud song came over the speakers.

"What kind of music do you listen to?" he asked.

"Nirinjan Kaur," I said without hesitation.

"Who's that?" I could tell he thought I was turning him onto some up-and-coming band.

"It's yoga mantra in Sanskrit."

"Cool," he said, looking at me like I had four heads before beelining for some other girl at the opposite end of the bar.

I felt like Julia Roberts in *Runaway Bride* when she finally realized what kind of eggs she liked. I also realized that I had just discovered how to lose a guy in less than three seconds and stay celibate indefinitely. It was truly liberating. Music was no longer an afterthought for me, or the question that left me feeling so awkward.

One afternoon in early April, I strolled into Harijiwan's class and barreled through the breathing exercises at such an alarming clip, my rubber band flew off my ponytail. I'm sure I looked like a crazy person with my hair swishing from side to side in every direction. But I didn't care. When class was over, I strolled past Harijiwan.

"Have a birthday coming up?" he asked.

In this moment, I realized that birthdays were a lot like periods for me. I always seemed to forget why I felt so off-center right before they struck, and then they would hit and I'd scream, "Of course!" Even though I'd been feeling pretty content with the current path I was embarking on, somewhere deep inside I must have been well aware that I was turning thirty-eight with no man in sight. And I'm sure this worried my subconscious a little.

Golden Bridge encouraged students taking a yoga class to bring a treat (like watermelon slices or vegan brownies) on their birthday to pass out after class instead of expecting to receive a treat from someone else on that day. Still, I suggested the Chateau Marmont for my birthday dinner celebration that year. Libby, Chloe, and Liz were all in teacher's training with me, but Annie, Kat, and Sloan were outside the yoga loop; and I could tell they were relieved I wasn't having my dinner at some ashram.

Chateau Marmont was a very "who's who" place. Unless you were in the company of some big movie star or movie director, you really couldn't get in. So I'm ashamed to admit that after all this spiritual work I would still want to go to a place like this, but their patio was hands down one of my favorite spots in L.A. and Chloe got us a reservation, so that was that. We had a long candlelit table under the arches—the best table in the house. We were just waiting for Annie, and our party would be complete. A couple of minutes later, she turned the corner and walked out. I did a double take when I saw who was behind her.

"MOM?" I ran up, sobbing.

"Happy birthday, darling," she said, holding me tight. *Why wasn't there a guy like my mom out there? Someone who loved me through thick and thin.*

We had the best night celebrating with great food and wine and champagne. For the first time in a while, I drank a little. After dessert, my friends passed out gifts to me. Kat gave me a really hip, navy blue top hat. As soon as I put it on, some older guy walked by and totally checked me out. "You just got a shout out from Harvey Weinstein," Kat said. I'd heard a couple of stories recently about this old fart and cringed. He was the powerhouse of Hollywood at the moment.

After opening gifts, I pulled a bag out from underneath my chair and passed each of my friends a wrapped CD I had burned them with one of my yoga meditations. I could tell Sloan was kind of weirded out, but none of that mattered. What mattered was that I'd never given anyone anything on my birthday, and the mere act of giving, no matter how small, felt really good. It was like my whole heart opened up. Then, of course, my mom secretly picked up the bill for dinner (I can assure you my friends liked that more than the CD meditation). Leave it to my mom to be a perfect yogi without even being conscious of it. She was amazing like that.

That May, a couple weeks after my last teacher's training weekend, Golden Bridge hosted a lovely graduation ceremony at the studio. Each student was called onto the stage and received a teaching certificate from Gurmukh, along with a strand of mala beads from this little girl who was sitting next to her, pulling them out of a big basket at random. She plunged her hand elbow deep into the beads after my name was called. "You get owange," she said through two missing front teeth.

I thought it was a good omen. Orange was my favorite color. I immediately wrapped them around my wrist as a bracelet to remind myself of the last eight months. I'd really come to depend on the built-in structure of yoga in my life. When you're required to be somewhere one weekend a month, you just show up. My happiness followed the discipline of my practice. As I walked off the stage that very last day, I was determined to keep up my yoga practice on my own.

What I wasn't sure I could keep up was my real estate career. It was 2007, and the real estate market was going down the drain. Mortgage companies were making it tough for buyers to get a loan, and nothing was appraising out. All over town, homes were being foreclosed on or in short sale. Sellers were really angry. It wasn't uncommon to walk into a bank-owned home and see holes punched in walls or kitchen sinks ripped out of countertops. It was tough, if not impossible, for me to keep a real estate deal together. I should have been freaking out, but I was so calm from all the meditation I'd been doing, one would think I was selling a house a day.

In June, Liz asked me if I would be her White Tantric partner at Summer Solstice in New Mexico. White Tantric yoga is a very intensive day of meditation that cuts through the blocks of the subconscious mind. It's done sitting opposite a partner in all white. Practicing just one day of it has been claimed to be the equivalent of doing ten years of meditation. This seemed farfetched to me, and my dad had just invited me to join him in Florida that same week. I needed a break from all the yoga and called Liz and told her she'd have to find someone else. Then I went home and threw all my whites into a suitcase instead of my bikinis as if I had no choice in the matter. All my teachers warned me that this could happen, that my conscious mind would find a reason not to do White Tantric while my subconscious would decide it was time to give it a whirl.

Upon our arrival at the ashram in New Mexico, a Sikh woman with two long whiskers coming out of her chin checked us in at base camp. It was all I could do not to pull out my tweezers. "There's a wheelbarrow out front for you to haul your stuff up the mountain," she said, handing us our badges. Unlike me, Liz had made the wise choice to stay at the Motel 6 at the bottom of the dirt road. Still, I turned to her hoping she might offer to help me set up my tent: no such luck. "I'm going to go check out the bazaar before heading back to the motel," she said.

As I maneuvered the wheelbarrow up a steep path in my Tory Burch flip-flops, I counted over three hundred tents on the mountainside. Each tent was on top of the other. Bonding with Mother Nature wasn't as romantic as I thought it would be. I settled on an area to the north of the porta-potties. After several failed attempts of setting up shop, I finally inserted the last fiberglass rod into the canvas and watched my tent rise from the dusty ground like a balloon. I thought it looked a little small for one person and consulted the side of the box. "Sleeps two," it read. I wasn't sure how this was possible unless you were a hobbit.

Liz snuck up on me from behind. "Want me to help you put your clothes away?"

"Put them away where?" I snapped, wiping my forehead of sweat and searching for a shower. Liz turned around on her right heel and walked away.

I covered my ears, but the sound of a man's voice rippling in song across the mountain seemed to be getting closer. I unzipped my tent and saw a long bearded fellow with white hair zigzagging through the campsite, strumming on his guitar:

"Rise up. Rise up, sweet family dear. A time of the Lord and remembering, love is here. Love, love is all you'll say, if you awake and rise up right away."

I forced myself out of my sleeping bag and slipped into my Uggs and followed the other campers down a dirt path. It was only 3:00 a.m., but people were filing into the tent in droves. I plopped myself in between two Sikh men who looked like they were two hundred years old. I wanted to wrap myself inside their bearded chins to get warm. It was absolutely freezing outside. I closed my eyes: *Why had my life pulled me here? These people were so different from me.*

"You are exactly where you should be," a voice responded in my head.

But I don't want this to be where I should be. Last summer, I was sleeping between two thousand thread-count Egyptian cotton sheets at a billionaire's beach house and, this summer, I'd settle to be in between the beards of two old Sikhs? This SUCKS! I hate you. I should have been married by now.

"Well, you are all alone," the voice in my head said.

The two old men looked at me.

Oh, God! Did I just have this conversation out loud?

As *Japji* began to play in the background, I forced myself to close my eyes, hoping for some peace from all this chatter.

"You will always be alone!"

Too agitated to find any stillness, I got up and walked out.

Fuck White Tantric.

Once the sun rose over the mountain, it was too hot to hide inside my tent any longer. I peeled off my Patagonia and threw on a tank top. White Tantric was starting in one hour and a long line of people had already formed outside the main tent. I figured I might as well try it and made my way there to get a good seat. Close to a thousand people would be attending, and everyone wanted to sit in the middle of the tantric tent where there was more protection from the sun and wind and dust.

When Liz approached forty minutes later, she was carrying a yoga mat, an Indian blanket, water bottles, a collapsible chair, leg contraptions, eucalyptus patches, and throat lozenges to get her through the day. Throughout teacher's training, Liz was always the person everyone wanted to sit next to because she was prepared for everyone else's worst-case scenario.

I always wondered how she managed. I didn't even own a proper makeup case. However, today I realized we weren't so different: I was encumbered by my thoughts. Liz was encumbered by her things.

We found a spot one row out from the middle and rolled our mats in half and sat down facing each other in a cross-legged position, knee to knee:

"Move back a little, you're putting too much weight onto my leg."

"Scoot to the right, the sun's in my eyes."

"Come forward, our knees need to touch."

You'd never know we were best friends from our bitch session. Then a mediator came onto the stage and guided us through a series of breath exercises, and we relaxed. Luckily, so did everyone else under the tent, as Liz and I weren't the only ones here with a few problems. There were over a thousand people sitting shoulder-to-shoulder in long straight rows searching for peace in a pose.

As Liz and I stared into each other's pupils for the sixty-two-minute meditation, it occurred to me that Oliver and Jake had never looked into my eyes for this long before. My eyes pooled with tears. Perhaps this was what true intimacy was all about? A few minutes later, I felt a rush of electricity pulse through my body and my arms started to vibrate. I got a little scared but kept my gaze on Liz, telling myself *I am safe*. Then Liz's face started to melt. I assumed my mind was playing tricks on me the same way it did during a long driving stretch when I thought I saw water ahead and would blink only to realize it was just pavement; but Liz's face continued to melt until suddenly…

Liz was Japanese.

My immediate thought was reincarnation. It made sense. Liz was drawn to Japanese culture. She had modeled in Japan and spent a lot of time there. She even told me once that her husband found Japanese women attractive. But as I continued to stare at a Japanese Liz in her late forties with straight, silky hair that fell at her chin, I wondered why my vision of Jake getting down on one knee to propose couldn't have come to fruition instead. All the self-help books had promised that visualizing what I wanted in my life would make it so. Oh well, I guess I would have to settle for a Japanese girl instead. When the meditation was over, I looked at Liz.

"For whatever it's worth, if there's such a thing as past lives, then you were definitely Japanese in one of yours."

"And you a young blonde boy," she replied without flinching.

A vision of this boy's mother popped into my head, so I sent her a blessing and told her I was okay. As strange as this whole experience was, I felt a sense of peace wash over me the minute Liz told me she had seen my past life, too. It felt like a validation somehow. I felt like I got an answer to one of life's unknowns. Although I would never be able to prove that reincarnation was real, I knew one thing was true: I felt a lifetime lighter.

After the final meditation on the third day of White Tantric, the facilitator shared a few closing words from the stage. "As you prepare to leave here tomorrow and go back out into the world, please leave everything behind you in Espanola, the fear, the doubt, the heartache."

The following morning, I felt like I was floating on a cloud. It was as if someone had unscrewed the top of my head, turned me upside down, and shaken out all the garbage from my brain. I took in the million-dollar views from my campsite before disassembling my tent. It had been a worthwhile trip, but I was ready to go home and tackle whatever lay ahead—a new boyfriend, perhaps?

Liz and I planned to stop for lunch in Santa Fe on the way to the airport. The food at the ashram had been very limited—celery soup and bananas for breakfast, a raw vegetable burger for lunch, and mung beans and rice that volunteers scooped out of large community buckets with their hands for dinner. A combination of ingredients, which, I had been told, promoted a deeper meditative experience. As we headed out of Espanola, I turned around to take in the mountains one last time before Liz hopped on the exit toward Santa Fe in a few blocks. The way the light beamed out of the clouds in thick streams, which the locals refer to as "God Light," was truly magnificent.

"Leave it all in Espanola," I whispered to myself, peaceful as the Dalai Lama. Then I turned back around and took in the open stretch of highway that lay ahead of me and inhaled deeply as Liz and I coexisted in perfect, comfortable silence.

"Turn around!" I yelled, out of nowhere.

"What?" Liz asked, understandably perplexed.

"Turn around," I replied.

"Why?" Liz said.

"Because I have to go!" I screamed, horrified I might not be able to hold in whatever had just over-taken my stomach.

Liz, no longer confused, pulled a rock-star U-turn off of the exit and headed back toward Espanola. There was not a gas station or fast food restaurant in sight.

"There!" I pointed at a Bank of America.

As Liz sped into the parking lot, I squeezed my bottom together. To my dismay, the bank was closed.

"What am I going to do?" I asked with humiliation.

Without saying a word, Liz pulled a box of handy wipes out of her bag, shrugged her shoulders, and smiled.

"It's not funny," I yelled, grabbing the wipes from her hand.

There was a small batch of trees to the right of the bank. I dashed into them, pulled down my sweats, and squatted.

A voice in my head said, "I told you to leave it all behind you in Espanola."

A couple of weeks after leaving New Mexico and returning to Los Angeles, I woke up in the middle of the night with a horrible anxiety attack. I was shaking really hard and my heart was racing. After all the yoga work I'd done over the last year, I thought I was done with all that. I hopped out of bed and opened a window for some air. Then I closed the window because I had this bad thought that I might jump out of it.

You are still all alone, Ms. Yoga.

I remembered that one single pill of Xanax Chloe had given me over a year ago that I hid in the organic fruit bowl—just in case—and ran down the hallway. As I turned the corner into the kitchen and flipped on the light switch, I was met with the single magnet on my chalkboard that my gut had told me not to take down: FAITH.

Tears fell down my face as I searched the bottom of my fruit basket until I saw a single white pill. I pulled it out and held it up toward the kitchen light to make sure it wasn't some random old vitamin or an Advil. It was so small compared to the vastness of the word I'd just been met with on my chalkboard. I leaned on my counter for support. By now, my heart was really racing.

"God, I know you made me in your image and likeness. You designed me. Therefore, I must have come without all the crap I quite literally thought I left behind at Bank of America just last week. So, here's the rest of it! Take it. It's yours. I'm done with all this bullshit."

I threw the Xanax down the drain and turned on the garbage disposal. Then I poured myself a glass of water and took a couple of deep breaths. I could feel the warmth come back into my legs. I had just overcome a very dark hole within my own mind. For the first time in my entire life, I was overwhelmed with this single thought: ***I am enough***.

I walked back to my bedroom, slithered under my covers, and slept more soundly than I ever had. I had finally heard and connected to my true authentic voice.

It was an unusually cold, dark winter by LA standards, but with the unprecedented frost that took over the orange trees that season, as my chi continued to rise, my pain didn't run as deep or stay as long. Instead, I noticed that the weight stayed off and all the chardonnay fell by the wayside, just like Gurushabed had promised it would that day I stumbled into his class a hopeful skeptic, and he said, "Just add yoga."

Although it would have been nice to be with a significant other, I was excited to head back to (you guessed it...) Chicago to see my family for the holidays. My mom was hosting Christmas at our lake house an hour outside of the city. It reminded me of Nantucket this time of year, with lots of wheatgrass all around and white picket fences everywhere. On a clear day, you could even see Chicago across Lake Michigan, with its waves often frozen in place.

On Christmas morning, my sister, step-dad, two step-brothers, and I all strolled into the living room one by one and took a seat on the couches next to the fireplace; then we waited for my mom to make her way to the Christmas tree and pass one gift at a time to each of us. It was like the giving tree. They just kept coming. After about two hours of this, my mom pulled the final gift from underneath the tree—a manila envelope—and approached me.

"For moi?"

"You know I always save the best gift for last," she replied.

"Or at least the most poignant," I said, recalling the present I received last year at this time. *He's Just Not That into You.* Hoping whatever was inside would not reveal how my life wasn't working for me, I pulled out a single sheet of paper with Gurmukh's picture on it. The words *India Yatra* (spiritual journey) were written underneath her, and underneath that, my mom wrote: "I am most excited about your trip to India."

A couple of months earlier, I had told my mom about how Gurmukh takes students to India with her each February. I also told her I was a little unsure if I would ever be brave enough to do the whole ashram thing, which included sleeping on a wood plank and meditating at 2:30 a.m. every day while in Amritstar.

Tears cascaded down my cheeks. Only now, my tears were not over some guy I hoped would be more into me. They were for this amazing adventure that awaited me.

"Mom?" I said.

"You are ready," she replied.

I arrived back in L.A. with a suitcase, a laptop, a paper bag full of loose ends, and a purse overflowing with too many receipts. Yet, somehow, I managed to find my keys at the bottom of my purse. Lugging everything across the courtyard and up a flight of stairs, I felt really, really single. I had taken a cab home from the airport. It would be good to get inside and organized. I inserted my key into the doorknob, but it wouldn't open. That's when I noticed that the top lock was bolted and pounded on the door with frustration. I was so tired, and none of my pals were back from Christmas break yet. Plus, I was a little confused because I didn't own a key to the bolt.

Pulling out my cell phone, I called my landlord, William, and explained the situation. He told me to call a locksmith, which he would reimburse me for. He'd had the heating system serviced when I was away and said that one of his guys must have accidentally locked the top bolt. I kept a phonebook out on the balcony and searched for a locksmith in the yellow pages. They told me it would be about forty-five minutes, so I went to get my mail and walked back upstairs and began sifting as I waited. There was a red Christmas card envelope with warning messages written across it: "Beware Before Opening!" and "Proceed with Care."

Flipping the card over, I saw it was from Oliver's MOM. Although we had remained friendly, I'd blown off her invitation to get together after we broke up. It was just too painful for me. I ripped open the envelope: a family Christmas photo that included Oliver's mom and new husband, Oliver's brother with his wife and kids, and Oliver with the same girl from New York, sitting on his lap, kissing him. She had clearly gotten the memo on Paris Hilton's "fashion" look, her short skirt, sporting gorgeous legs.

I opened the card and read the preprinted words: "Oliver and Rachel got married in a surprise ceremony. Friends thought they were showing up for a Christmas party when, in fact, it was their wedding." Underneath that, Oliver's mom handwrote: "Just bringing you to speed."

ARE YOU KIDDING ME? Flabbergasted, I looked at the family photo for several minutes. Then I did something atypical. Instead of calling all my girlfriends to stir up the drama and vent and cry and scream, I plopped myself into a cross-legged position and began chanting until the locksmith arrived forty minutes later. Like Harijiwan had promised, the words just poured out of my mouth when I needed them.

CHAKRA SIX & SEVEN

John and Me
Spring 2009

"To be yourself in a world that is constantly
trying to make you something else is
the greatest accomplishment."
—Ralph Waldo Emerson

That March, I asked Chrissie to go to lunch at La Scala. She was in the process of moving to New York full time to be with Ben. They had just gotten engaged, and I was desperate to spend as much time with her as possible. The restaurant was packed when we arrived. While we waited for a table, Chrissie slid her sunglasses on top of her head, creating the perfect headband for her gorgeous, dark blonde locks, and scanned the room. A pretty brunette with milky skin, large brown eyes, and cute dimples was eating at the bar. Her name was Christine. She was a former soap star that Chrissie knew through a mutual friend they shared. We made our way back to say hello.

"I heard you got engaged," Christine said, exchanging hugs with Chrissie, her four-carat engagement ring blinding me.

"And I heard you had a baby," Chrissie replied.

"Johnny," Christine confirmed proudly, as she pulled out her cell phone and scrolled through an array of photographs of her adorable baby boy.

Christine asked me if I was married yet. Of course, I told her no.

"Are you dating anyone?" she asked.

"I haven't been with anyone in close to a year," I said.

Smiling coyly, she told me she had this guy to set me up with named John. He was one of her husband's best friends, a great golfer, and from Chicago. She went on and on about his incredible looks. "Beyond gorgeous," she said. Chrissie nudged my arm encouragingly. "There is one thing though," Christine said. "Are you a Christian?"

"She's a Catholic" Chrissie blurted, before I could answer.

Yeah, a recovering one, I thought, as Chrissie shot me a look that screamed: *No guy will ever relate to chanting Sanskrit mantra. You should go with this.*

"Yes, I'm Catholic," I said.

Appeased by my confirmation, Christine reached for her cell phone and asked me for my number to pass on to John.

That following Thursday, I blew out my hair and borrowed a green Tori Burch sundress from Chrissie. For the first time in months, I felt *dressed.* I also felt like a virgin again. Sex and men had been the furthest things from my mind. A "beyond gorgeous" guy stood outside the restaurant entrance talking into a headset. If this was John, all the breakups I had endured over the past decade may have been worth it. They led me to Adonis.

"John?" I asked, a little intimidated.

He smile-nodded, pointing to the headset inside his ear and mouthing that he was on hold with the gas company. Feeling more awkward by the moment, I waited. Finally, a hostess walked up and escorted us to our table. John was still on hold and hadn't said a word to me as we sat down. *Who stays on the phone with the gas company on a first date?* This guy wasn't for me.

"So, I heard you're a hardcore Christian," I said, without waiting for him to hang up.

Retiring his headset to the table, he looked me directly in the eye. "God's a big part of my life," he said with a smile.

Something inside me softened. For the next hour, we talked about yoga, religion, and work. John was waiting for a position to open up with an internet company his friend was about to launch. Before moving to L.A a couple of years before, he was in sales in Dallas, where he had bought and sold a few properties. It seemed like he was in transition—in a good way. As we continued chatting, a handsome guy passed our table and checked John out.

"What are you looking at?" he said in an annoyed tone. It didn't seem very Christian. I pointed out that Jesus's best lady friend was Mary Magdalene, a downright floozy, and he still loved her. "You know, you're right," John said. "Every day, I ask God to refine my heart."

I liked that: *refine.*

It occurred to me that whatever one uses to get themselves to refinement—Buddhism, Christianity, Downward-Facing Dog, or the Yankees—if it takes your heart in a good direction, then it's working on some level. Again, something inside of me shifted. For the first time in a long while, I felt a little spark.

John shot me a flirtatious wink. "You sure are pretty," he said.

The following day, John called and asked if I wanted to grab a quick bite at this organic café on Little Santa Monica and Crescent. Impressed that healthy, organic food was on his radar, I told him I could be there in twenty minutes. Because it was errand day (a.k.a., I-don't-have-a-single-real-estate-client-to-show-a-house-to-today), my look was Bohemian-casual: no shower, hair up in a half ponytail, half bun because I couldn't bother with either and divided the difference, and a *Love Yourself* t-shirt with ripped jeans.

When I entered the restaurant and saw John standing there in a suit, I had to make a concerted effort to keep my jaw shut. Twirling my hair with my finger to contain myself, I walked up to the counter to order a vegetable roll. He reached across the bar and put his hand on top of mine.

"Want to be my date at a big wine tasting dinner I was invited to in three weeks?' he asked.

I wondered how I was going to fit back into the world of dating and merlot. Grabbing a drink together was a big part of the dating process, and I was thinking of giving up alcohol for good. Perhaps it was time to find a happy balance again. I told him I'd go.

A couple of days later, John invited me to the Bel-Air Country Club to play tennis. I had never been there before but knew it was one of the most prestigious clubs in Los Angeles. Howard Hughes had once flown his airplane onto the course to charm Katharine Hepburn, whose house was off the eighth hole. Wearing my best whites (no, they weren't my yoga whites), I drove through the large iron gates and met John on the tennis court. He was practicing his serve and approached the net and kissed me. "I've been waiting to bump lips with you," he said. I told him I had been, too.

After hitting balls for an hour, John asked me if I wanted to go out to dinner. He suggested a place in Brentwood and told me to leave my car there. He'd drive me back to get it afterward.

On the way to the restaurant, John reached over the console to hold my hand. "I think we should wait to have sex," he said. He told me it wasn't for religious reasons. It would just be nice to get to know each other first. Before my yoga practice, this may not have resonated with me, but now it made a lot of sense. I was taking care of myself in a new way and liked the idea of getting to know someone before jumping in the sack.

Ruminating on what he said, John withdrew his hand from mine to shift his car into fourth gear. I was a little nervous at how fast he was driving but didn't say anything. Everyone thinks they're immortal in the early throes of falling in like. Especially John, who was now shifting down into third while darting in and out of cars down Sunset, twenty miles over the speed limit.

Over the next couple of weeks, it was *JUST* lunch. It was easier to avoid sex if no alcohol or moon was involved. John made me feel cared about in a dozen different ways. At the Bel-Air Country Club, we drove around in a golf cart and fed the ducks between his practice swings. He made me homemade chicken soup with organic carrots and brown rice when I got sick midweek. And he gave me ten percent of his cash earnings from a round of golf he'd won that Saturday. "Here, go buy yourself something pretty," he said, peeling a few twenties off a roll of cash.

But not sleeping with John was starting to feel a little weird to me. I'd had enough celibacy. So, that Wednesday, I invited him over for a romantic candlelight dinner. I spent hours creating the perfect ambience for seduction: a roaring fire, a sheepskin rug strewn on the floor, and the perfect bra and panty set peeking out from underneath my button down.

When John arrived, I lowered the lights a little more. The fire inside me was raging more than the one inside my fireplace. I noticed he had a little satchel/backpack on his shoulder but didn't think much of it. Suggesting he relax on the sheepskin in front of the fire, I poured him a glass of red wine and sat down next to him, a little bit of my bra peeking out. Reaching into his knapsack (I hoped for a condom), he pulled out a worn black bible and opened it to Paul.

"Can I read you one of my favorite passages?" he asked.

"Sure," I said, tucking my bra strap back into my shirt and rolling my eyes behind his back.

The day of the wine tasting, I bought a short sweater dress and a pair of black suede boots that came above my knee. It was the sexiest look I'd sported in over two years. As I headed to John's house that evening, I wondered if I'd overdone it. My dress hiked up to my underwear line every time my car made even the slightest traverse down Sunset Boulevard. Luckily, when I walked through John's door, his jaw dropped open. "Baby, you look sexy!" he said, slithering his body up against mine. It was the most body contact we'd ever had.

A couple from John's church was hosting the tasting at Divino, a restaurant less than a block from John's condo, so we walked over. Three other couples were already seated at the table. A sommelier approached to pour the first pairing of wines: a 2006 Dalbiere, Fattoria and Tergeno, Fattoria Zerbina. Everyone began sniffing and swirling and gargling the wine with the kind of reverence with which I'd recited my daily mantras during Sadhana. Picking up my Dalbiere, Fattoria, I inhaled deeply into the glass. Everyone at the table stopped and looked at me because it was so loud. "Too much yoga," I said, hiding my red face in my red wine. This seemed to appease the group, who went back to their wine.

Ten minutes later, the first course came out, accompanied by a 2004 *Torre Di Ceprarano, Magnum Fattoria Zerbina.* Good Lord, these names were harder to pronounce than the Sanskrit mantras once were for me. Maybe if I participated in wine tasting long enough, their names would one day roll off my tongue and become part of my vernacular the way the mantras had. Inhaling into my third glass, a little less breathy this go around, I took another big swig.

"Too Licorice-y," I blurted, wine coming out of my mouth. Again, everyone at the table stopped and looked at me. "Sorry, I haven't had anything to drink in like a year," I slurred. "I've been meditating."

John grabbed my hand under the table and chuckled. I picked up my little pencil with my free hand and made a smiley face on his tasting menu. I was so dizzy as a new round of 1994, 1998, 2001, and 2003 Marzieno made its way around the table, I had no idea if I'd get through it. Yet, somehow, I managed to tell John the 1998 was my favorite. He picked up the pencil and drew a little heart next to 1998 on my tasting menu so I'd remember. Grabbing my pencil, I scribbled on my menu:

"Will you still like me if I barf at your house?"

"I'll like you Moore" he wrote back. Moore was John's last name. I leaned in and gave him a peck. Then I almost blacked out.

When we got back to John's, I was in no condition to drive and asked him if I could sleep on his couch. He said a bed would be more comfortable and suggested we sleep fully clothed in his room instead. I wasn't about to argue. A bed sounded divine right about then. I could sleep forever I was so toasted, but before my head hit the pillow…John slipped off my dress. We started to go for it. Two seconds later, John stopped abruptly, and this weird heaviness and guilt descended on him and the room.

The following morning, he brought me breakfast in bed: oatmeal stewing in maple syrup and fresh-cut fruit. He was really peppy and sweet and said he was sorry if things got a little strange the night before. I chalked it up to too much to drink.

The country was going into recession. My real estate career was at a standstill. No one was buying houses. Instead, everyone was short selling them or in foreclosure. All the stores on Sunset Plaza were vacant and had *for rent* signs on them. Gas was over five bucks a gallon. People all around me seemed nervous, but everyone was putting on a brave face, including me. I wasn't surprised when John told me the start-up where he'd been expecting to begin a new career wasn't starting up after all. He seemed devastated, even if he tried not to show it. Wanting to be supportive, I agreed to join him at the church service he'd invited me to near the airport.

John wanted to make sure we got to the church on time because he'd heard that over six-hundred people attended the service. Shooting in and out traffic like a maniac down the 405 Freeway, I held onto the little handle above the passenger seat for dear life. But when he crossed over four lanes of highway from the carpool lane to make the exit at sixty miles-per-hour, I lost it.

"Slow down!" I barked. He snickered, but I was not amused. *What overtook him as he drove?* His emotions seemed to shift with the gears, from frustration to all-out rage to compassion.

A large black man, who looked more like a bouncer with his walkie-talkie than an usher, led us to our seats. Parting a crowded aisle like Moses parting the Red Sea, he made special arrangements through his walkie-talkie for us to sit in the VIP section of the church—front row, center. Perhaps it was because we were the only white people among the four thousand at the service?

Struck by all the vibrantly colorful outfits and women in hats, a soprano from the gospel choir struck me with something else: a "C" note she sang with such sweet perfection, I felt my heart vibrate just like it did when I heard the gong being struck at yoga. As the congregation began to chant "Jesus" in unison, I could feel a sensation of heat pulsating through me in much the same way I felt my chi rising up my spine on an inhale while chanting Sanskrit mantra. No matter the faith, I realized, the act of devotion encourages the God/energy/Jesus/love to flow. I continued to go with John to this service several more times, while keeping up my yoga practice, too.

One Monday morning, about three weeks later, after we had gone to sleep snuggling and kissing, I rolled over to give John a good morning kiss, but he wasn't interested. He was glaring at something in the far right corner of my bedroom. I followed his gaze to my little black Buddha, perched on top of a stack of magazines that had accumulated some dust on my dresser.

"Everything okay?" I asked gently.

"I just wish Jesus could be enough," he sighed.

I wanted to poke my eyes out and scream at the top of my lungs "me, too!" But I didn't. "It's not like I worship it," I replied as he shot my Buddha stink eye.

"I just worry about the dark places it comes out of," he said. "The people who made that statue worship false gods, making you perilously close to worshipping false gods, too."

Although my yoga practice had provided me with a deeper appreciation for Jesus than any of my catechism classes in Catholic school, I didn't want to rock the boat over a statue and offered to take it down. I wasn't a Buddhist. John said he didn't need me to do that. Then he hopped out of bed, revealing his eight-pack abs and gave me a peck on the cheek.

"I just worry about you, baby," he said.

You didn't seem too worried about me when you pulled off of the freeway exit going ninety miles-per-hour last Sunday.

The following Friday, I walked into my bedroom to change out of my work clothes and noticed that my Buddha was missing. A lot of my household chores had slipped because I had started sitting a bunch of open houses for other agents earlier that week. Perhaps the dirty dishes in the sink, wet towels in the bathroom, and pile of dirty clothes strewn across my bedroom floor had distracted me from noticing? I checked to see if my statue might have fallen behind my dresser. When I realized it hadn't, I reached for the phone and dialed John.

"Did you take my Buddha?" I demanded.

"No," he said with a chuckle. "Maybe he's in your dirty laundry."

"My dirty laundry?"

"C'mon, Amy. Lighten up. It was a joke."

"Let me call you back," I said.

After devoting a whole year to tapping into my higher chakras, I just thought that I wasn't going to fall down anymore, that it would be impossible to get involved with another man who wasn't right for me. Yet, here I was. Sitting down on my yoga mat next to my bed, I inhaled into this conundrum and asked God to reveal what the blessing and the lesson in dating John could be. As a side note, I also asked if He wouldn't mind finding me a title for this book.

After an hour of breathing in and out with no direct answer, I was famished. Meditation always left me hungry. Fantasizing about a frozen pizza or bean-and-cheese burrito, I hopped off my yoga mat, walked into my kitchen, and opened my freezer, where I couldn't believe what I found instead.

"He put my Buddha in the freezer!" I screamed.

Quickly pulling my Buddha out of the cold, I rubbed his poor frostbitten scalp with my hand. He was so cold I thought he'd crack in half as I placed him in front of the sunny bay window above my kitchen sink. Then I pulled over a stool and sat down. Perching my elbows on the countertop and resting my face in my hands, I stared at my statue for several minutes. Harijiwan mentioned that the higher I reached, the harder I could fall. It was easy to stay enlightened at Golden Bridge, but then I came back down the proverbial mountaintop and stepped back into the world of La Scala and wine and John.

As I watched my Buddha thaw in the light, beads of water dripping down his head, I realized that I, too, had allowed a part of myself to freeze the morning I offered to take him down. It dawned on me that my whole journey had been a process of disconnecting and reconnecting to myself—a process of freezing and thawing. Yet somehow, in all of those moments of thawing and freezing over the last decade, I also realized with each guy I moved **on to**, I simultaneously ascended **into** another chakra.

With Richard, I'd discovered that the security of home has nothing to do with living in a big, fancy house. Feeling at home in myself was the first step to getting grounded and being secure, a theme very inherent with the first chakra.

With Matt, I experienced aspects of my sexuality I never had before. Although this exploration of my womanhood had been wonderful in many ways, I realized that giving this piece of myself away could be depleting, too, because I had neglected to maintain a balance with the other things in my life that were important.

Luckily, while dating Oliver, I got my mojo back by reconnecting with all that determination and self-grit associated with the third chakra; but I also learned that self-determination and being determined to change someone else are two very different beasts. Oliver, in many ways, had been honest about where he was at in our relationship, and I chose not to believe him, or—worse—I believed I could change him with all my determination. In the process, I wasn't being true to myself or owning what I wanted: a man who wanted to start a chapter with me in it.

Along came Jake, a perfect man on paper, who I hoped with all my heart would heal my heart from all its old wounds, only to find that my next heartbreak would push me toward the yoga once and for all, allowing me to truly heal my heart (fourth chakra) and connect with what made Amy tick—a voice I could only discover by getting still with myself for a while—all very reminiscent of the fifth chakra.

And then there was John, the man who entered my life for a millisecond to give me a test run as I reentered life with all that yoga knowledge, which I temporarily dropped, reinforcing that it was time to trust my intuition (sixth chakra) for good, and not waste any more time on the wrong guy.

Each break up had indeed been a breakthrough (seventh chakra, enlightened). Each man had played a very important part of my journey up. A little piece of frost glistened off my Buddha's head in the sunlight, reminding me of the story Gurmukh had shared about diamonds. Before a diamond is a diamond, it is a piece of coal. Without heat and pressure, that's all it will ever be.

It was a crisp, cool day without a cloud in the sky. My female neighbors were outside in the courtyard preparing to eat a lovely lunch next to the koi pond around a big wooden farm table dressed in a white linen tablecloth and purple petunias. As I joined them around the table, I found solace in their warm greeting. I didn't have a four-carat ring on my finger or my name up on the marquee. But because things hadn't turned out exactly as I had hoped, I was forced to grow. Like that little piece of coal in Gurmukh's story, I, too, had evolved into the best version of myself.

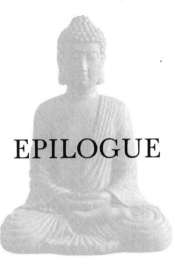

EPILOGUE

S hortly after dating the guy who put my Buddha in the freezer, I started teaching yoga and holding workshops in various cities. During my meditations, I kept seeing—in my mind's eye—a vast, open space of land with unending blue sky and boulders and more sky. I wondered if it was some place I'd be visiting or moving to but didn't give it much thought. Then, a year later, after an adventurous decade plus in L.A., I found myself in Scottsdale, Arizona, where I still happily reside today with my son and cherish my best role yet: mom.

Although I get back to L.A. often to do yoga and see friends, it occurred to me while driving north on Pima Road to this majestic place called Desert Mountain (where I spend a lot of time working alongside some of the top real estate teams in the country with my marketing job) that the only thing surrounding me was blue sky and boulders and vast amounts of open desert land. I realized it was the exact setting I saw in my mediations years earlier.

"Guess this is my new La Cienega!" I chuckled, remembering the L.A. boulevard I'd traveled daily for work. I'd come a long way to get to my current road and…it was all sort of perfect.

Made in the USA
Monee, IL
08 October 2020

44335092R00159